Beyond the Science Fair

Creating a Kids' Inquiry Conference

Wendy Saul, Donna Dieckman,
Charles Pearce, Donna Neutze

With Megan Dieckman,
Holly Buck,
and Leesa Green

HEINEMANN
Portsmouth, NH

Heinemann
A division of Reed Elsevier Inc.
361 Hanover St.
Portsmouth, NH 03801–3912
www.heinemann.com

Offices and agents throughout the world.

The authors and publisher with to thank those who have generously given permission to reprint borrowed material:

Figure 7–1: from *Nurturing Inquiry: Real Science for the Elementary Classroom* by Charles R. Pearce. Copyright © 1999 by Charles R. Pearce. Published by Heinemann, a division of Reed Elsevier, Inc. Portsmouth, NH. All rights reserved.

Figure 7–2: from *Science Workshop: Reading, Writing, and Thinking Like a Scientist*, 2/e by Wendy Saul, Jeanne Reardon, Charles Pearce, Donna Dieckman, and Donna Neutze. Copyright © 2002 by Wendy Saul, Jeanne Reardon, Charles Pearce, Donna Dieckman, and Donna Neutze. Published by Heinemann, a division of Reed Elsevier, Inc. Portsmouth, NH. All rights reserved.

This material is based on work supported by the National Science Foundation under Grant No. 0439116. Any opinions, findings, and conclusions or recommendations expressed in this material are those of the authors and do not necessarily reflect the views of the National Science Foundation.

Library of Congress Cataloging-in-Publication Data
Beyond the science fair : creating a Kids' Inquiry Conference / Wendy Saul . . . [et al.] with Megan Dieckman, Holly Buck, and Leesa Green.
    p. cm.
  Includes bibliographical references.
  ISBN 0-325-00734-9 (alk. paper)
  1. Kids' Inquiry Conference. 2. Science projects—Congresses. 3. Science—Exhibitions. 4. Science—Study and teaching (Elementary)—Activity programs. 5. Inquiry-based learning. I. Saul, Wendy.
Q182.3.B49 2005
372.3'5—dc22   2004027988

Editor: Robin Najar
Production editor: Sonja S. Chapman
Cover design: Night & Day Design
Cover photograph: Will Chapman, taken by Rich Beauchesne, *Portsmouth Herald*
Compositor: Argosy
Manufacturing: Louise Richardson

Printed in the United States of America on acid-free paper
09 08 07 06 05 RRD 1 2 3 4 5

Contents

Appendices 133

    A. Application for Hands-on Display

    B. Application for Presentation

    C. Biographical Data Form

    D. Certificate of Participation

    E. Chaperone Letter

    F. Checklist for Host Institution

    G. Checklist for Teachers

    H. Congratulations and Acceptance Letter

    I. Inquiry Grant Proposal Application

    J. Journal Article Guidelines

    K. KIC Is Coming Announcement

    L. Moderator Letter

    M. Parents' Guide to KIC

    N. Parent Survey

    O. Participant (Student) Survey

    P. Presentation Blurb Guidelines

    Q. Presentation Evaluation Form

    R. Presentation Guidelines

    S. Progress Report

    T. Publicity Announcement

    U. Teacher-Student Contract

    V. Inquiry Investigation Plan

Acknowledgments

Sometimes a person gets an idea for a book, sits down, and writes it. Not so with most books in education—and this is no exception. So, let's begin our acknowledgments here:

First, there were the people we think of as Kids' Inquiry Conference (KIC) pioneers. In 1993 Charlie Pearce (who taught in a rural school) met Veronica Stokes (an inner-city teacher) through the NSF sponsored Elementary Science Integration Project (ESIP) and began planning the first conference held at the University of Maryland, Baltimore County. We needed another school involved so Barbara Bourne, then coordinator of ESIP, convinced Susan Wells, a suburban teacher, to join the group. We thank them for their imagination as well as their innovative ideas. But none of this would have happened without the support and encouragement of our NSF grants officer Susan Snyder.

Over the years many teachers, students, and other onlookers—scientists, parents, administrators—have participated in the program as presenters, moderators, or audience members. The many successes of KIC are directly attributed to all of their hard work and enthusiasm through the past ten years. Of special note, we thank Phil Sokolove, Professor of Biology at University of Maryland, Baltimore County, who has been a supporter of KIC since the beginning and contributed a piece to the second chapter of this book offering his observations from a scientist's perspective.

There is a special group without whom this book would not be written—teachers Betty Lobe, Maureen Hoyer, Karen Pearce, Deb Galinski, Susan Wells, and Jenny Zmarzly. They not only participated in the project over the years, but have been unfailing in their willingness to share insights and help us learn from their experiences with the initiative. One lovely fall weekend, as the sun shone outdoors we met in a basement unpacking years of experience with the program. And as the teachers talked and recollected, our able team of KIC novices—Leesa Green, Sutton Stokes, Holly Buck, and Jill Hutchison—took notes and then wrote up all that they were able to capture . . . and there was a lot!

Our KICs have always featured a keynote speaker. Twig George, children's author and friend to the project, deserves special mention for her ongoing support and many great talks—about swimming with sharks or heading north to Alaska to search out new book ideas. She's been an inspiration to students and adults alike. And we have always given away science goodies to participants—there is no better source for these as well as great speakers (at least if you are in the DC area) than NASA. Special thanks to Don Robinson-Boonstra.

Although we had a good fix on what it meant to be a KIC teacher, learning more about how KIC worked for students presented a special challenge. Megan Dieckman, now a brave college student majoring in chemistry, called the boys she worked with as 4th graders in her KIC program (described on pp. 78). Lo and behold, they were willing to get together to look back at their experiences. It is with great appreciation that we thank Stewart Wolfe, now a student at Washington University in St. Louis, Chase Gilbert, now a biology major at University of Maryland, Baltimore County and Joe Conroy, now a student at Salisbury State University in Maryland.

I am sure that we are missing many thank yous, but we cannot think about this book without expressing our special appreciation to Holly Buck and Leesa Green. Whenever we were stuck they seemed to come through. Holly, now a writing student in Boulder, Colorado, did interviews and the opening chapter's newspaperlike description. Leesa, now a teacher (but formerly a very good English major) helped with editing and contributed greatly to the chapters on classroom ideas.

Without all of these folks, we would surely not have been able to share the KIC experience with you.

1 *The Kids' Inquiry Conference: An Overview*

Laura Barston loves to chew gum. She can tell you about the cinnamon-flavor crystals in Big Red, the taste-bud-popping fruitiness of Juicy Fruit, or the coolness of the mint in Ice Breakers. And with the guidance of her teacher, this fourth grader turned her love for chewing gum into a scientific inquiry. Now, standing before an overhead projector in a classroom at the University of Maryland, Baltimore County, Laura presents evidence she has collected herself that indicates which of these competing brands really has the longest-lasting flavor. She has learned a little more about chewing gum—and a lot about the scientific process. Her round face, framed with straight brown hair, looks out at the audience of thirty of her peers; her expression is serious. By the end of her presentation, Laura is visibly more comfortable with her pointer and her overheads. She can add public speaking skills to the list of things that she has developed through this inquiry.

This presentation, one of perhaps forty presented at the annual Kids' Inquiry Conference (KIC), is as much a state of mind as a place or an event. Laura's class is one of five classes from around the Baltimore area who have come to the college campus to share their work in progress. Their teachers, who grew tired with the standard science fair format and the rigid trifold notion of the scientific method it promotes, joined up with a university-based organization called the Elementary Science Integration Projects to take part in an alternate form of science work—a noncompetitive format that focuses on student inquiry and sharing.

What does a Kids' Inquiry Conference look like? The following is a snapshot of a day at KIC as it unfolds, with a few close-up peeks at some of the participating students and their work.

At 9:30, the first buses arrive. The exuberance of the students and the careful planning on the part of the university staff turn what could become a logistical nightmare—signing all the kids in and assigning them to their rooms—into a well-organized and cheerful welcome. Talking excitedly, the students receive their color-coded name tags, which direct them to one of four rooms (red, yellow, blue, or green) for each of the four sessions of presentations. After delivering their presentation materials to their designated place, students and guests file into the University Center and settle down to listen to a welcome address from a UMBC professor. Then they make their way to classrooms for the presentations.

Each room has a moderator that announces the presentations. Student presentations take place simultaneously. Two sessions are scheduled for the morning and two in the afternoon. In one room, presentations are focused on the topic of light.

Rachel and Amanda investigated whether sunglasses could completely block light, a question that arose when they were shopping for new shades for the summer. Kevin and LaToya, students at an urban school that was planning to plant a garden, investigated how much light different plants needed to grow. Both pairs of students talk for about ten minutes and then respond to a host of questions from fellow students, about two-thirds of whom are unfamiliar faces. After their presentations, one of the adults in the room shares her observations about the packed ground where students walk and where nothing grows and asks if any of the students have a garden where nothing grows. This sparks a lively discussion about gardens, sprouting tales of drowned cantaloupes and overwatered watermelons.

The session's moderator, a teacher in training, notes a connection between the botanical presentation ("Shady Science") and the previous presentation on sunglasses: could plants still grow through different types of lenses? One girl raises her hand and says she thinks that they could. "Well, feel free to take it and run with it," the moderator suggests. Thus, inquiry begets inquiry, and science is born. The generative, creative energy is almost palpable, and with gentle guidance from the moderators, the students' urgency to relate their gardening stories is transformed into new ideas.

After the concurrent morning sessions, the action moves to the demonstration tables that rim the perimeter of the university ballroom. Students who elected to develop hands-on presentations display their projects and chat one-on-one. While students may be tense during the formal presentations, the hands-on activities students have set up allow their unbridled enthusiasm to shine.

A sign, drawn with markers, reading "Hi I'm Ericka. My topic is mealworms. Please Come!" is placed above Ericka's table. It goes on to say,

"Remember—egg, mealworm, pupa, beetle. Answer for a chance to win: Do mealworms eat apples?" Little slips of paper are provided for kids to scrawl their answers on, while the mealworms creep around in their jar, unaware that their fate is up for grabs.

"Swoosh," a project that investigated the correlation between one's basketball experience and the number of baskets one makes, has several students clamoring to shoot tiny basketballs into a toy basketball hoop and prove that science and sport are intermeshed.

Another popular hands-on activity is "Which Chip for Your Dip," a creative mingling of the ever popular snack food and an innovative experimental design. Frustrated with chips that break during dipping, students devised a testing stand where weights were placed upon a chip until it broke. Free samples are distributed in the name of science to attract passersby, and the chip-testing gadget snags students' curiosity. The verdict? Sun Chips beat out Doritos, thanks to their ripples.

While half the students visit hands-on tables, the other half take tours of the university's science labs, since many of them have never set foot on a college campus before. Students then switch activities after lunch, which is sandwiched in between the hands-on presentations and campus tours.

At KIC, real-life investigations bring on all sorts of unforeseen problems. Unlike the science proffered in most science kits, KIC is not neat. It requires (and teaches) revision and creativity. Science is not cut-and-dried. It is part of a living, breathing planet where everything is connected and one inquiry leads to the next and where inquiries get tangled. Science, like life, is messy, even moldy.

On the hands-on table marked "Dyeing," a student features zippered plastic bags with colorful berries and the swatches of fabric that were dyed with them, in shades of lavender and pink. The materials spell success, but the board notes: "One problem I had was that the berries got moldy and started to smell."

This messy, authentic experimentation and the accompanying student-to-student interaction may be the essence of KIC. However, kids also get the opportunity to hear what a professional scientist has to offer. Because KIC is an attempt to connect students' own inquiries to those engaged in by real scientists, the two afternoon sessions are followed by a closing keynote presentation in a university lecture hall by a practicing scientist or science writer from the region.

Dr. Frank E. Hanson, a biologist at UMBC, comes to the podium.
"Hey, gang!" the professor begins, beckoning for the students to reply. "What is your favorite food?" he asks. Predictably, a boy replies, "Pizza!"

Another student shares her least favorite food: "Black-eyed peas!"

Then the professor says, "Suppose you didn't have any eyes?" A collective gasp arises from the crowd. The tall, graying professor has captured the undivided attention of a hundred elementary school students who are at the end of an exciting, even exhausting, field trip experience. Dr. Hanson continues, "How would you pick your food?" He explains that in his lab, scientists are working with simple animals that don't have eyes but still have "specific kinds of food they like and don't like." The inquiry is, then, How do simple animals find their food? The lights dim, and Dr. Hanson's assistant, Raj, projects a video feed of the materials on the podium onto a screen so that everyone can see the action that's taking place there. The podium is playing host to tobacco worms, which are munching on six different types of green leaves. As Dr. Hanson reminds the audience, "Caterpillars can't tell us what they like." He tells the students that at the end of the keynote lecture, they'll see if [the worms] made a choice.

Interesting, but what does all this talk about choice of diet have to do with real science? Plenty, as the professor explains. At his lab, scientists are working to understand more about how creatures know what foods are useful for an organism and which are poisonous.

Not only have students experienced the pleasures of doing science, but they have met someone who does this kind of work for a living. However, before the students must make their way to their buses, there is one last thing to do: the drawing for Ericka's mealworms.

The lucky winner's name is Samantha. The dark-haired girl emerges from the lecture hall with her mealworm prize, contained in a cleaned-out baby food jar. What is she going to do with these creatures? She doesn't know, but she opens the jar to show anyone willing to look. "It's a little thing, man," Samantha says, with a trace of marvel in her voice. "See?" she asks, adjusting the jar to allow for a better view. "It's so little." Samantha might not have a plan for her little pets yet, but the sense of wonder in her voice is audible.

Wonder, when properly cultivated, provides the fertile ground upon which inquiry may sprout and bloom. KIC does not tell students how to "do" science, but it does invite them to participate in the pleasures of science. And it does help them see science in a different way—as dynamic, interactive, noncompetitive, and *alive*. At its best, KIC helps students see the world in general, and science in particular, as a bit more wonder-full.

2 *The Evolution of KIC*

We hope the previous chapter answered the question What is a Kids' Inquiry Conference? but it probably generated many more questions that you are now wondering about. How did KIC get started? What are the goals of KIC? How is it different from a science fair? How does a Kids' Inquiry Conference support the standards that govern the curriculum? Why on earth would I want to do this? In this chapter, we will address these very valid and frequently asked questions.

Everybody Loves KIC

Everybody seems to love the Kids' Inquiry Conference. Kids love it because they have a real opportunity to talk with others about what they have been doing, and others—be they other students, teachers, or visitors—listen with interest. You don't go to KIC to garner awards or even to celebrate successes. Rather, attendees are there to find out about the questions other presenters have and how they have gone about addressing those questions. They are also excited to share their own explorations and to see how their peers react. Those not formally presenting in sessions have brought with them a variety of science challenges and activities. KIC is basically viewed by students as fun.

Science educators love the event because it represents one of the few authentic opportunities students have to showcase and observe inquiry in action. By attending various sessions, engaging in hands-on activities, and talking with presenters, it is possible to capture a bird's-eye view of the range of student-initiated activities a school system supports. As one adult visitor at a KIC program noted, "I've been to a lot of field trips before, but none where the kids *were* the field trip." At a successful KIC conference, the room literally hums with engaging science.

Surely parents love KIC; it's the "no more tears" version of a science fair. That is, there is no pressure on parents to create high-end trifolds. Every student who puts in the effort gets to shine. Opportunities for

5

thinking and stretching are unlimited. And the work is done by the students themselves.

And teachers, too, love KIC. Well, perhaps not at the beginning when they're nervous about how they are going to be able to fit one more thing into the curriculum, fulfill the ever increasing reading block, and still get the lunch money counted. But they love KIC when they see how it benefits the children in their charge.

A Scientist's View of KIC

I had read the Elementary Science Integration Projects grant proposal, and I was on the ESIP advisory board. However, I did not understand the full impact of the ESIP program until I observed and participated in the first ESIP Kids' Inquiry Conference.

First, a bit of background: I had graduated with a degree in physics from the University of California, Berkeley, and obtained a Ph.D. from Harvard University in the area of biophysics with a specialization in neurobiology. Then, after a few years as a postdoctoral fellow in biological sciences at Stanford University, in 1974 I joined the faculty in the Department of Biological Sciences at the University of Maryland, Baltimore County. I taught classes in introductory biology, general animal physiology, and neurobiology, did research and published papers about behavioral neurobiology, and eventually received tenure (1978). At no time did I receive any professional training whatsoever in how to teach. Nevertheless, I thought I was doing a pretty good job of teaching. My lectures were well organized, my tests were hard but fair, and the histogram of my students' exam scores usually produced a normal-looking distribution. Unfortunately, no matter how hard I tried to be interesting and even entertaining (sometimes), not many students in my large lecture courses (about 260) looked interested in what I had to tell them.

Sometime later I found myself working in the Office of the Dean of Arts and Sciences as an associate dean. In that position I had a chance to meet and speak with many faculty members outside of biology. One of the faculty members I met was Dr. Wendy Saul. I remember that one day she phoned me and asked if I would read a grant proposal she had written. I was, she said, a "real" scientist who she thought would appreciate what she had written and who could provide a reasonable critique. After I read the proposal, I did my best to offer a few suggestions that I thought might help clarify some parts of it, but, as I recall, I neglected to mention that I had no idea of what the term *metacognition* (which she had used in the proposal) meant. The reviewers at the National Science Foundation knew what *metacognition* meant and thought the ideas in the proposal were worth funding. After the grant was awarded, Wendy asked me to be on the advisory board for her project. That was how I ended up at the first KIC. I represented a "scientist" who was interested in helping young children learn about science. Most of that interest, of course, was due to my association with the ESIP teachers and to the patient "instruction" offered to me by Wendy. At least I eventually learned what *metacognition* meant. And I also watched how the ESIP program taught elementary school teachers how to regain a sense of wonder about the world around them and how to help young children learn to explore that world scientifically. The trick was to let children ask questions and then, rather than answer their questions directly (teacher-as-expert), help the children learn how to find the answers themselves (teacher-as-guide-and-facilitator).

So, back to the first KIC—there I was in what was normally a cafeteria for the commuting UMBC students, and racing around me were elementary school children who could not wait either (1) to show other children—and any adult who would listen—about what they had discovered through their own investigation of a question that they had or (2) to learn about what questions and investigations the other children had done. My recollection is that there were two elementary schools in which the children got bored with telling each other (those in the same school) about what they had done (i.e., about their questions and how they had gone about answering them). When the teachers at the two schools met at a regular ESIP program meeting, they each reported the same complaints from students who had only each other to talk to and who wanted a wider audience. Wendy offered to organize the first KIC so that students from the two schools could report to each other about their science investigations. KIC was a chance for the children to explain what they had done and what they had learned to a new group of interested peers. What excitement!

Wendy had also asked an outsider to visit KIC—a newspaper reporter. After the reporter and I were introduced, she asked me, as a scientist, "What do you think about ESIP and KIC?" I replied that that ESIP was really a wonderful program because it let teachers off the hook. They did not have to know everything and did not have

continued

to be embarrassed when their students asked a question they could not answer. Instead, they were able to say, "I don't know, let's find out together." And I thought that KIC was a wonderful example of how excited students became when they learned how to find the answers to their own questions. "After all," I remarked, "these kids have learned how to ask good questions about the world around them, and good questions are at the heart of good science."

"So, when exactly," a little voice shouted inside my head, "did *you* ever encourage *your* students to ask questions about the world of biology?" I never did. I just walked into the lecture hall and began to talk about some topic or other. I never encouraged my students to explore the world around them. Whenever they did manage to raise their hands and ask a question, I (the "expert") usually had an answer for them . . . or, if not, I said I would "look it up and come back to the next class" with the answer. Now I let them do the work. "That's a wonderful question," I will say to a student. "I don't know the answer to your question, but I wonder if you would try to find the answer for us, and then come back to class and share what you have found." Almost always, the student does find an answer that he or she is willing to share.

They, and I, have learned much over the years since my first KIC. I learned how to let myself say, "I don't know the answer." My students have learned, with my encouragement, how to ask good questions and then find an answer themselves. Sometimes I can help by suggesting where they might look for information, but mostly they succeed with little or no help from me. Some work alone, while others enlist the aid of their fellow students. I feel good because I have made their questions an important centerpiece of my teaching. They feel good, because, like the elementary school children at KIC, they have an audience of their peers to whom they can report the answer they have found—an answer that the teacher didn't even know. The first KIC was fun both for the children and for me. It was also my first learning experience in how to teach the "doing" of science rather than just the facts. Good questions are, indeed, at the heart of good science.

Phillip Sokolove
Professor of Biology
University of Maryland, Baltimore County

The Origins of KIC

In many ways, the story of how KIC began provides a window into its philosophical underpinnings. In the summer of 1992, about thirty teachers participated in a National Science Foundation–funded summer teacher institute sponsored by the Elementary Science Integration Projects (ESIP). Susan Snyder, an NSF grants officer at the time, was there for a site visit, and one of the participants, fifth-grade teacher Charlie Pearce, joined her and ESIP Project Director Wendy Saul for lunch.

"So how did this particular project get funded?" Charlie asked.

"All of the proposals we received in this solicitation were reviewed, and the proposal for this program was judged among the most worthy," the grants officer replied.

Those of us in ESIP had spent a lot of time that summer thinking about authenticity, autonomy, and community that summer (see Saul et al. 2002 for a more fulsome discussion of those topics). Perhaps because of his interest in authenticity, Charlie began thinking through what the classroom analogue of the grant review process might look like. Would it be possible to have students turn in proposals and, if a student's proposal were reviewed favorably by the teacher and the student's peers, give the student time and resources to pursue independent work in science?

Several days later, Charlie looked up from what he was doing and asked, "And how does anyone know that the proposed work was accomplished successfully?" Clearly the grant proposal idea was still on his mind, but a piece was missing. How are the results of research shared? Does someone just come in and grade a scientist's work? Certainly not.

We talked together for some time about the milieu in which scientific results are presented: that generally science is seen as work in progress, but that at logical stopping places, when results are available, the scientist of record presents findings to her or his colleagues, who then ask questions about the idea itself, about the processes involved in gathering data, and sometimes about the data. And then, if the scientist still feels somewhat confident about the work that was shared orally, he or she submits these findings to a journal, where even more people read about the work and replicate it and build upon the findings in their own labs.

A conference . . . a real science conference in which students would present their own inquiries . . . the idea was intriguing. But where would the audience come from? Was it possible to create a conference for students that seriously mimicked the kind of conferences in which practicing scientists participate? Could we avoid the pitfalls of a science fair—students prematurely grabbing for hypotheses, more to fill the left side of the trifold than to investigate a personally meaningful question; librarians searching frantically with anxious parents for ideas that would work; nervous children who worked perhaps harder than ever before only to come home with nothing to show for their efforts and believing, finally, that science is for "winners"?

That year (1992–93), Charlie was working in a rural school with a 100 percent Caucasian student population. But sitting next to him at the summer institute was Veronica Stokes, a teacher from inner-city Baltimore whose urban class was 100 percent African American. And behind them sat Susan Wells, a superbly well-organized teacher from suburban Maryland. The three educators, with varying degrees of reluctance and significant help from the ESIP staff, began to plan the first Kids' Inquiry Conference (KIC).

As in a conference for adult scientists, concurrent sessions were organized around topics that bore some relationship to one another. Whenever possible, we tried to involve students from different schools in each session, both as presenters and as audience members. It was our goal, in part, to use science as a shared interest and to provide an opportunity for a diverse student population to talk and listen to one another.

There was, however, one frustration expressed by students again and again: they had wanted to attend all of the sessions but had been forced instead to choose from concurrent sessions. This, in effect, meant missing out, and it appeared that no one wanted to miss anything! It was from this simple frustration that the *KIC Journal* was born. If students could publish their work—much like proceedings at an adult conference—attendees could look back and see what they missed. They would also have a record of what had transpired, a memento of their own work and that of others with whom they had interacted that day.

The idea of KIC has grown significantly since 1993, but the conference itself, from a student's point of view, remains basically the same. Rather than increase the number of students at a given KIC, we have chosen to have additional KICs each year. Some of these events have a focus—once we had a KIC for young children in which two schools shared their investigations of water—while other KICs target a particular age group. Still, in the best of circumstances, the non-science fair atmosphere dominates. (See Figure 2–1.) And when we do see students sliding toward the science fair model, we have adults around to run interference. Moderators rephrase "What is your hypothesis?" interrogations from the audience into questions like "What did you expect would happen?" that facilitate meaningful discussions about the work that is being presented.

Not Just Another Science Fair! How KIC and Science Fairs Compare		
	KIC	**Science Fairs**
Questions	Curiosity driven	Hypothesis driven
	Students' questions can and often do change	
Research	Less structured, more organic	Follows a sequenced "scientific method"
	Classroom centered—many opportunities for cross-curricular connections (reading, writing, communication)	Usually extra-curricular and done outside of the classroom
	Students aren't "done" when it comes time to present	The presentation is the end goal
Presentation	Process oriented	Product oriented
	Goal is documentation and analysis of an investigation	Goal is to prove or disprove hypothesis
	Story driven and idiosyncratic	Follows a predetermined template and specific requirements
	Students share next steps and new questions	Students present "conclusions"
	Noncompetitive; peer evaluated	Competitive; judged and ranked by adults

Figure 2–1. KICs versus science fairs.

The Goals of KIC

From the outset, our goals for the conference were ambitious. We wanted to provide several opportunities for children:

- *Children would own their inquiries.* Student interests were sometimes driven by the topic; that is, they identified a phenomenon that they wanted to know more about and designed a way to learn more about it. In other cases, a desire to apply a particular process, like using their newfound interest in battery power, was key to their KIC project idea. In still other cases, KIC proposals seemed to grow from a personal aesthetic; for example, a child wanted to build something that looked cool to build. In all cases, the inquiry became personalized.

- *Children would interact with students from different schools who had common interests.* Many youth groups, both secular and religious, recognize children's interest in meeting others their age with whom they share interests. This desire to move beyond the walls of the school seems to create just enough tension to push students to do their best without dwarfing their enthusiasm, an all too common effect of playing to adult judges in the typical science fair.

- *Children would view science as a dynamic force in their own lives.* KIC projects begin with an immediate, concrete interaction with phenomena. In exploring these phenomena, students learn that they are capable of exploring and interrogating the world in which they live. Science, in this sense, is no longer relegated to a team of experts, but rather becomes part of the world they are capable of learning more about.

- *Children would communicate in authentic ways and for authentic purposes.* As students keep track of their findings, write notes to document ideas about what might be happening, share ideas with one another, write proposals and contracts, and prepare to share their understandings and data with other students, the practical usefulness of those skills become patently clear.

- *Children would consider, critically, the credibility of their own research and the research of others.* We, adults and children alike, succeed only when we are able to step away from our work and revise. There is no more important skill than the ability to decide when and where revision is necessary or helpful. Although this is perhaps the most important goal of learning, far too few opportunities to practice the art of critical reflection and discourse are available in schools.

- *Children would draw upon the discoveries of other students to enhance their own research.* Although we talk about the importance of cooperative learning and recognize that in the workplace cooperation is an increasingly necessary attribute, school cooperation has too often been reduced to mechanical turn taking (e.g., you are the materials monitor, I am the secretary), largely directed by the teacher. KIC provides authentic opportunities for students to become intrigued with, borrow from, and cite the research of others. Through this process they learn to value the work of those who came before them and see their own work as contributing to knowledge at large.

KIC and the Standards-Based Curriculum

Standards-based education is the watchword of our times. No teacher or principal or superintendent is unaffected by standards. Standards are driving curricular reform, teacher education reform, and materials development. In order to talk about acceptable or excellent practice, we are asked to identify those qualities that signal excellence (or sometimes minimally acceptable) classroom instruction. And the defined goals are back-mapped into activities. Four hundred fifty-seven goals too often lead to 457 discreet activities and 457 measures for success.

But the truth is that a single learning activity can address a large number of goals and standards. Said more colloquially, both students and teachers can walk and chew gum at the same time! To address each standard separately will lead to a monstrous curriculum that cannot be realistically met. Participation in KIC helps students meet both science and literacy standards, and many teachers have borrowed time from both their language arts and science blocks to prepare for the event.

Science standards fall into numerous categories, but content standards seem to be getting the lion's share of school attention, perhaps because they are easiest to address and to measure. It is fairly easy, for instance, to have students describe the life cycle of the butterfly or recognize the difference between a food chain and a food web. But, in truth, such tasks are more akin to a vocabulary lesson than to a science activity that promotes scientific thinking and the purposeful manipulation of materials. More worrisome is that the very first content standard, the standard that supports all others, is the Inquiry Standard, and it is too often being ignored.

The National Science Education Standards, developed by the National Research Council (1996) state that "students at all grade levels and in every domain of science should have the opportunity to use scientific inquiry and develop the ability to think and act in ways associated with inquiry, including asking questions, planning and conducting investigations, using appropriate tools and techniques to gather data, thinking critically and logically about relationships between evidence and explanations, constructing and analyzing alternative explanations, and communicating scientific arguments" (105). KIC presents a perfect opportunity for students to learn and practice these very skills.

In terms of the literacy standards, KIC involves practicing and honing reading, writing, and oral language skills (see IRA and NCTE 1996). Students are exposed to and work in different genres and for different audiences. In looking at performance on standardized tests, American students do fairly well understanding literary texts, but when it comes to reading and writing exposition and procedural text, a more worrisome picture emerges. KIC provides authentic opportunities to work with both of these forms. A more thorough discussion of how science and literacy standards are supported by KIC can be found in Chapter 8.

Justifying KIC

My friends in advertising tell me that in selling an idea, you should limit yourself to three to five talking points. To practice, they create "elevator speeches," that is, presentations you could deliver as you rode with a prospective client between the third and fifteenth floors. They need to be short, punchy, and ideally, memorable.

What follows is a list of brainstormed talking points. You can surely expand this list by brainstorming with other KIC enthusiasts. As an exercise, think of the list this way: Which three to five points will play best to *your* audience?

KIC is beneficial in myriad ways. For example, KIC:

- promotes ownership of questions and investment in science
- engages students in personally meaningful searches for data and explanation
- engages students in authentic writing tasks and provides opportunities to demonstrate and discuss observations and inference making
- provides opportunities to critique and learn from others
- offers opportunities to revise in science, to do it again
- is multidisciplinary—meets various reading, writing, and science goals
- gives your students an opportunity to meet and work with students from other schools
- encourages high expectations and celebrates good work
- requires students to translate from one form of knowing to another, for example, from notes to oral presentations to journal articles, allowing them to revisit and better understand material
- showcases multimodal forms of communication (graphic, written, oral)
- promotes critical reading and reading for a purpose
- teaches ways to question one another and offer constructive criticism
- offers differentiated learning opportunities for students of differing skill levels and differing learning styles
- inspires and motivates so that students want to learn more
- values application of learned material
- offers new roles for both teachers and students
- provides living proof that there are many ways to share science
- promotes critical thinking
- values a combination of originality and reasoning
- allows students to be producers and decision makers, not just consumers of science
- presents science as an active process—the opposite of ready-made and immutable

Looking Back, Looking Ahead

For many teachers, KIC has now become a classroom tradition. The stories of KIC are passed along from one year to the next. As the children read the KIC Journal articles written by students from previous years, the continuity of our science community is extended. The children develop a different sense of themselves as readers and authors. The children want to become a part of the KIC tradition. They anticipate the KIC applications and work hard to submit their best effort. It's almost as if science is being exploited because of its natural interest and draw for the children. But the effects are powerful.

More than ten years have passed since the first Kids' Inquiry Conference. Those children we remember as KIC pioneers have grown and scattered. Yet the impression and lasting effects of KIC have been profound. We hear from students like Meg, a contributor to this book, who presented at KIC when she was in fourth grade. Her enthusiasm and commitment serve as a model for others as she communicates with current students through her "Ask Meg" section of the KIC website (*esiponline.learnserver.net/kic*). Other students have written from college or have visited to express how meaningful the KIC experience was for them.

One of our initial goals with the early conferences was to set the groundwork to assist other teachers who wanted to have their own inquiry conference elsewhere. We valued the assistance of the university through ESIP in getting this project started but realized the true value of our work would be in providing a model for others who had no such assistance. We knew that three or four teachers on their own could plan and conduct a conference for their students, but we wondered if it would be possible to sustain such an effort amid all the other responsibilities of classroom teachers. Our hope is that this book will help provide the support for those teachers who are convinced that their students will benefit from participating in KIC. Not only do our contributing authors provide the nuts and bolts of actually pulling off a kids' conference, but the classroom strategies from KIC teachers provide encouragement for those who may wonder along the way how this idea can possibly work.

If your students are asking questions and probing possibilities; if you are encouraged by the National Science Education Standards and their commitment to inquiry; if you can imagine the value of youngsters coming together as scientists, then KIC may be for you and your students.

References

International Reading Association (IRA) and National Council of Teachers of English (NCTE). 1996. "IRA/NCTE Standards for the English Language Arts." Retrieved from *www.readwritethink.org/standards/index.html*.

National Research Council. 1996. *The National Science Education Standards*. Washington, DC: National Academy Press.

Saul, W., et al. 2002. *Science Workshop: Reading, Writing and Thinking Like a Scientist*. Portsmouth, NH: Heinemann.

3 *The Road to KIC: A Classroom Story*

Charles Pearce

There are multiple paths to KIC. Each teacher who takes his or her students to the conference prepares them in any number of possible ways. Described here is one teacher's story.

It may be comforting for the classroom teacher to know that long before the first day of the new school year the children have unknowingly been preparing for an inquiry conference. These kids may never have heard of KIC or thought of themselves as scientists, but their experiences have been scientific in nature. For years, the children have been doing the things that all scientists do. In their play, they have been observing, exploring, and manipulating their environments; they have been asking questions and making predictions. Their collected data have led to all kinds of discoveries. Most importantly, our students have been using what they have discovered to ask more questions and make more discoveries. At the beach, in backyards, in basements, and in parks, children's play has been important science. They bring the results of these investigations with them into the classroom.

My challenge, as a classroom teacher, is to create an environment in which the scientific expertise of each child is valued. By doing so, I am setting the stage for an authentic inquiry conference. But although the children enter the classroom as scientists, there is much to be done before they are ready for KIC. The first day of the new school year is not too early to begin capitalizing on the strengths the children already possess.

Those first-day opportunities are important to set the tone for the science inquiry that will follow. For the classroom teacher, early inquiry activities are an exciting way to really grab the interest of the incoming students.

Day One

UV Beads

Of the many ways to get students enthused about the start of a new school year, my favorite has been UV beads. These little white beads indicate the presence of ultraviolet light by changing colors. Inexpensive and easy to find, UV-detecting beads begin as a mystery and always lead to questions and investigations. The following story about Joe and the beads, as told in *Nurturing Inquiry* (Pearce 1999), is a classic.

As the students arrived that first day, I gave each six little white beads and some plastic gimp string. I told the students only that the beads were a first-day gift. I mentioned nothing about their special powers. Many of the students wondered what kind of a gift six little white beads could be. I told them it was the best I could do and that they just might find those little beads interesting. As the day began, the beads were put away and forgotten, not really the most memorable of gifts. But I knew all that would change. It happened when Joe made his amazing discovery.

By midmorning, the beads had taken on far more significance. Joe had found that by clicking them back and forth on the gimp string, he could make the beads change colors. Students around him were all clicking their beads, delighted with the changing colors. Joe became a hero for discovering the secret of the beads. Meanwhile, across the room, disappointed students were clicking their beads with no resulting change in color. I pretended to be as confused as they were.

It wasn't until recess that students discovered the real truth about the beads. Outside in the sunlight, the other children began making discoveries of their own. Of course, the changing colors had nothing to do with clicking the beads. In the classroom, Joe and those around him were seated by the windows. On the playground, the beads changed colors not by being clicked but merely by being exposed to the sun. As we discussed the events of the first day, the class realized that Joe's theory *was* valid until more data were gathered. It was then that the questions about the beads really began to flow and the question board began to fill up.

The Question Board

Earlier in the day I had introduced the class to the question board, a laminated piece of oak tag on which students were invited to write their own questions. By the end of that first day, questions about UV beads were numerous. *Will the beads change colors on a cloudy day? What if the beads are under water, will they still change? Will sunscreen keep the beads from changing?* These and other questions led some students to go home that evening and try experiments of their own. (See Figure 3–1 for a sample question board.)

The first-day read-aloud really got the question board started. I was reading the first chapter of *A Dolphin Named Bob*, by Twig George. Read-aloud is a great time to think aloud. As I read, I stopped to ponder some questions that came to mind and asked a student volunteer to write my questions on the question board. It wasn't long before the kids really

Student Questions from the Question Board

1. How does a camera work? Mary   *What kind of camera works best?*

2. If I crack a seed in half and plant it in two different places will it grow two plants? Chris

3. What is inside a battery? Emily

4. What if UV beads are under water, will they still change? Corey

5. What other things did Pascal make besides the triangle? Samantha

6. What makes the seasons change? Cierra   *When do our seasons change?*

7. Will sunblock keep UV beads from changing color? Samantha

8. Are there other sources of UV light besides the sun? Megan

9. Was the Trojan War real? Adam

10. What does friction have to do with hurricanes? Suzanne

11. How does television work? Madeline   *What if I looked at a TV screen with a magnifying glass?*

12. How do clouds form? Mary   *How many kinds of clouds are there? Can I shine a light on a cloud at night?*

13. How do meteors form? Ben

14. How old was Fibonacci when he died? Joey

15. Why does the earth spin? Katie

16. Is there a scale to measure tornadoes? Joey

17. Why does a sailboat float? Renee   *How much cargo can different sized boats carry?*

18. Will the drinking bird continue to go up and down if the glass of water is taken away? Allison

19. Can you test the pH of everything? Tim

20. When you look through the smoke from a grill, why does everything look fuzzy? Alyson   *Can I read while looking through smoke?*

continued

Figure 3–1. Sample question board

21. How big is the sun? Tim

22. Is there a chance a meteor will hit the earth soon? Nicholas

23. How do radios work? Mary   *How far can walkie-talkies transmit?*

24. Why is there gravity? Shannon

25. Why are clouds white? Madeline   *Do all clouds bring rain or snow?*

26. Is there ever a time when there are no clouds in the sky? Allison

27. How big was the biggest meteor ever to hit the earth? Ben

28. What happened to comet TT? Timmy

29. Why is there no gravity on the moon? Katie

Italicized questions are testable questions suggested during class discussion.

Topics: cameras, batteries, Pascal, Trojan War, television, boats, pH, number systems, meteors, simple machines, Earth, seasons, the Moon, snow, tornadoes, comets, Fibonacci, drinking bird, hurricanes, plants, gravity, the Sun, clouds

Testable Questions _____   Research Questions _____

Figure 3–1.   (continued)

caught on. Soon, students were asking permission to write their own questions on the question board.

At the end of that first day we were already laying the groundwork for an inquiry conference. The kids had begun to ask their own questions and they were already thinking about investigations that might answer those questions. Over the next several weeks my role was to put into place an array of *question engines*—activities, ideas, and opportunities that would lead to more and more questions.

Question Engines

Anything in the classroom that leads the children to ask their own questions is a question engine. First-day question engines around the classroom might include

The UV beads

The read-aloud: High-interest science stories provide opportunities for question modeling by the teacher. Ideas for read-aloud books are listed in Chapter 11.

The question board

A classroom microscope: I prefer a child-friendly Brock microscope placed on the edge of my desk with no directions or suggested activities. After a day or two, someone will discover it and ask to look at some things through it. Questions always follow.

Tornado tubes: Children are intrigued by these connectors between two soda bottles that create a swirling tornado inside.

Beach sand display: This is a large sweater box filled with sand to simulate a beach. Shells, sea stars, beach glass, and any other items found at a beach (along with one or more field guides) provide a place for students to explore and wonder.

Indoor garden: A sunny windowsill is the perfect place to grow plants from seeds. Nothing seems to inspire as many questions as an indoor garden. A collection of *mystery seeds* (left over from summer) is not only interesting to examine (especially under the microscope) but also provide answers for the most basic of questions: *What kind of seed is it?* Grow-light tubes placed in an inexpensive shop-light fixture over a table will make for an indoor garden even in the shadiest of classrooms.

These and countless other possibilities will inspire questions and make for an exciting start to a new year. I don't discuss the idea of an inquiry conference at this early stage. It is just too far off. But I know that if I provide authentic opportunities for students to question and wonder, the children will spiral through inquiry experiences that will naturally lead to KIC.

Early Weeks

After the first few weeks, the question board is completely filled. As we value student questions yet often have no time to address them, the question board becomes a useful tool for recording those questions. When a question pops up in a class discussion that seems off topic or when there is simply no time to even consider new questions, the question board is a welcome place for a busy teacher to direct his curious students. The classroom teacher should never feel compelled to try to answer the questions. Usually the answers may not be readily known, and the teacher does not want to be the source of all answers anyway. Just having the questions published and displayed on the board is enough, at least early in the year.

When it seems the question board can hold no more, the questions are transcribed (perhaps by a parent or one or two students who have some time). I make copies of the questions and distribute them to the class, then I clean the question board, and we begin again. Next a class discussion ensues to analyze the kinds of questions that have been asked on our printed list.

Basically there are two types of science questions: *research questions* and *testable questions*. Helping the children distinguish between these questions will guide them toward their own investigations later. Research questions are questions that are best answered by a source other than the student. To answer these questions, one would research what someone else has already discovered. Books, the Internet, journals, and magazine articles are examples of answer sources for research questions.

Testable questions are those questions that are best answered by the students themselves, either by making observations or by designing investigations. These are the questions that fuel inquiry, the questions that have driven science throughout history. As students ask and pursue answers to their own testable questions, they are following in the footsteps of the scientists that have preceded them. The questions about UV beads are often testable questions. *How tall will the grass grow if it is not mowed?* and *Of an assortment of magnets, which is most powerful?* are also examples of testable questions asked by students. In our discussion, the distinction is an easy one. If a question is thought to be a testable one, we talk about what a student could do or observe to answer it.

The question board remains in use for the entire year.

The science curriculum is a powerful question engine that becomes valuable for inquiry as the year begins. The experiences in a traditional science class setting will lead to questions on the question board, especially if the teacher enthusiastically welcomes them. Not only will those questions help the teacher see what the kids are really thinking about, but they will help direct student-initiated inquiry investigations when the science unit is over.

Teacher-directed investigations, based upon the science curriculum, are introduced early in the year, as well as early student explorations with familiar materials from previous years. *Nurturing Inquiry* (Pearce 1999) contains a more detailed discussion about the logistics of these early forays into inquiry. The early explorations are generally informal, with an emphasis on questions, much class discussion, and a lot of modeling by the teacher. It is interesting how students value what is important to their teacher. A classroom teacher who is genuinely intrigued by science, reading, questioning, wondering, and finding out more will have a significant influence on the students.

Inquiry Explorations

Structured inquiry experiences early in the year are actually *inquiry explorations*, opportunities for the students to become familiar or reacquainted with a variety of materials and topics in an open-ended setting. Scattered around the room are inquiry stations, each a source of experiences through which the children can explore and discover. By trying out materials at each location, the children gain the prior knowledge necessary to develop their own questions.

Here are some sample inquiry station topics and the accompanying materials.

Magnets—An assortment of magnets with a variety of magnetic and nonmagnetic items. A cover sheet asks sample questions and offers some exploratory possibilities.

Boatbuilding—Several tubs of water along with materials to build boats: clay, aluminum foil, craft sticks, straws, rubber bands, and an assortment of weights. A cover sheet offers possibilities and a boatbuilding challenge.

Ramps and rollers—Small ramps with items that roll, such as balls and toy cars. Students are encouraged to measure distances of rolled objects and how they may be affected by different variables.

Structures—Toothpicks, marshmallows, dried beans that have been soaked overnight, straws, paper clips, and several weighted objects. Opportunities are available for students to build structures and see if they can support different weights.

Bubbles—Different bubble solutions are available for the children to assess. Size of bubbles, time aloft, distances traveled, and time before popping are suggested as possible sources of data.

Electricity—Wires, batteries, lightbulbs, and aluminum foil. Students are challenged to light the bulb or to try something new.

Marble roll—Paper towel tubes, thumbtacks, masking tape, marbles, and a stopwatch. With these materials, students are able to build a structure on a wall down which marbles travel. The challenge is for the marble to take as long as possible to reach the bottom without stopping.

Microscope—Simply a microscope with a variety of items to view.

This is merely a sample of the possibilities. There are many others, depending upon the available materials.

After the first few weeks of the school year, I introduce past issues of the *KIC Journal* as reading texts for the class. *KIC Journals* are collections of articles written by former students who attended and did presentations at earlier inquiry conferences. The articles provide stories of inquiry by students from previous years who now serve as role models. *KIC Journals* provide authentic science stories from students and also inspire new questions for current students.

End of the First Marking Period

Up to this point, the traditional science curriculum has been a source of prior knowledge useful for student investigations to come later, and it has been a rich source of questions, especially an increasing number of testable questions. The student explorations have been relatively informal, open-ended, and of short duration.

More Question Engines

Early *question engines* include UV beads, read-aloud books, a microscope, the indoor garden, and more. As the year progresses, additional question engines are introduced that inspire even more questions. They include

- science, math, social studies, and health curricula
- literature, read independently and in small groups
- materials for inquiry explorations
- discovery boxes
- outdoor experiences, from recess to formal visits to an outdoor setting
- visiting scientists and other classroom guests
- field trips
- *Kids' Inquiry Conference Journals* from past years
- the KIC website
- classroom animals
- the Internet
- newspapers
- videos
- science materials catalogs
- the classroom teacher and students, through class discussions or as they add more and more questions to the question board

Any activity or strategy that sparks questions can be considered a question engine, especially when the questions are valued, documented, and recorded for possible future use.

With the introduction of *discovery boxes*, the explorations become more investigative in nature and become far more focused. Discovery boxes are small plastic tubs filled with materials on a variety of topics, which might include magnetism, electricity, color and light, sink and float, boatbuilding, bubble solutions, mealworms, and structures. The materials are commonly found, especially in forgotten science storage cabinets. Often, when we've completed a science unit, I keep some of the leftover materials to create a discovery box. (A list of sources for materials can be found in Chapter 11.) In addition to the materials along specific themes, the boxes contain a discovery log in which students record questions and document discoveries (see Figures 3–2 and 3–3) and one or more books from the library related to the theme of the box. Absent from the discovery boxes are specific activities or directions. The idea is that students direct their own investigations based upon prior knowledge and their own questions. Skeptical readers may think this will never work. In reality, however, it has been used for years with students of varying ability levels. Not only do students respond well to the autonomy of an inquiry classroom, but they inspire one another with their questions, investigations, and discoveries.

Typically, students sign up for a particular box to be used during an upcoming fifty-minute discovery period. Before that discovery period arrives, the students must read through the log to see what others have done with the contents of the box and read the book(s) for prior knowledge and to develop several questions that the contents of the box might help answer. The students also review the contents of the box a day or two in advance in case there are other materials that may be needed. The teacher and students negotiate who will provide any additional needed materials.

A class discussion follows each inquiry period during which students from each discovery box report their adventures to the class. This discussion serves several purposes. First, it gets the kids speaking in front of the group. They are forced to conceptualize their questions, investigations, and discoveries. The discussion also helps advertise each box, especially for students who might otherwise not be interested in certain topics.

By now, I have invited the students to make entries in the *Book of Student Discoveries*, an ongoing record from year to year in which students record their observations. This book provides an authentic way to share the discoveries made with discovery boxes, independent explorations, and inquiry extensions to the curriculum. The language connection to science is increasingly being seen as a vital one as students record data on log pages, in independent dialogue journals, and in the *Book of Student Discoveries*. Once recorded, the information will be available for future research. (See Figure 3–4.)

Color & Light

Discovery Box

Some materials you may find in this discovery box include:

- mirrors
- flashlights
- color filters
- food coloring
- UV-detecting beads

- lenses
- prism
- fiber-optic cable
- watercolor paints
- colored markers

Directions:

1. Consider a question that you would like to answer. Think of your own or select from those below.
2. Read some of the log pages in this folder to see what other student scientists have discovered.
3. Begin a log page of your own.
4. Conduct your investigation.
5. Complete the log page you started with data and observations from your investigation.
6. Add what you discovered to the *Book of Student Discoveries*.

Some questions you may want to investigate:

- What colors are in a rainbow?
- How many colors are in white light?
- Is it possible to make light go around a corner?
- What happens when light is directed through a glass of water?
- How can I use mirrors to direct light?
- What if I combine two or more different-colored filters?

Remember: The best questions are your own questions!

Be curious!

Be creative!

Have fun!

Figure 3–2. Sample discovery box cover page

SCIENCE DISCOVERY LOG

Activity Light & Color   *Names* Kyle   Chad

Date 020416

What question did you try to answer? How many mirrors will reflect light before the light won't reflect light anymore?

Explain what you did to answer your question.

We set up 7 mirrors and moved them until light traveled from one to the next. Then we shined a flashlight into the first mirror and watched to see how many mirrors it would reflect off of.

Make a sketch of your experiment.

What did you discover today? The light reflects only 7 times. We tried 8 mirrors and it didn't work.

What new question are you curious about for another time? Will light reflect off more mirrors if we use a different flashlight?

Are you pleased with your results today? YES ✓   NO ___   NOT SURE ___

How would your group rate this activity? Great (10) 9 8 7 6 5 4 3 2 1 0 Terrible

Figure 3–3. A student's log page

Except for reading the *KIC Journals*, we do not talk much about an inquiry conference. But as the year continues I constantly watch the progress of the students. The more comfortable they are with asking questions, initiating their own investigations, recording data, and sharing their discoveries with one another, the more comfortable I am with the idea of an upcoming conference.

Midyear

By midyear the class has become a community of scientists. Students have been publishing their questions on the question board and sharing possibilities on finding answers. A variety of books have been placed at the question board, providing sources of possible answers and, more importantly, inspiration for further questions. The discovery boxes have been used during numerous inquiry periods when small groups of students have worked together to ask questions and use the materials to answer them. The students have been adding data to the log pages in each box and have been adding discoveries to the *Book of Student Discoveries*. Past *KIC Journals* have been read and students have learned

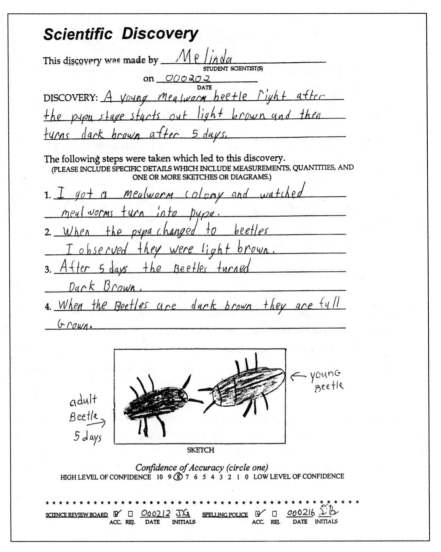

Scientific Discovery

This discovery was made by ___Melinda___
STUDENT SCIENTIST(S)

on ___000202___
DATE

DISCOVERY: *A young mealworm beetle right after the pupa stage starts out light brown and then turns dark brown after 5 days.*

The following steps were taken which led to this discovery.
(PLEASE INCLUDE SPECIFIC DETAILS WHICH INCLUDE MEASUREMENTS, QUANTITIES, AND ONE OR MORE SKETCHES OR DIAGRAMS.)

1. *I got a mealworm colony and watched mealworms turn into pupa.*

2. *When the pupa changed to beetles I observed they were light brown.*

3. *After 5 days the Beetles turned Dark Brown.*

4. *When the Beetles are dark brown they are full Grown.*

adult Beetle → 5 days

← young Beetle

SKETCH

Confidence of Accuracy (circle one)
HIGH LEVEL OF CONFIDENCE 10 9 ⑧ 7 6 5 4 3 2 1 0 LOW LEVEL OF CONFIDENCE

★ ★

SCIENCE REVIEW BOARD ☑ ☐ ___000212___ ___JG___   SPELLING POLICE ☑ ☐ ___000216___ ___SB___
ACC. REJ. DATE   INITIALS   ACC. REJ. DATE   INITIALS

Figure 3–4.   Page from the Book of Student Discoveries

about science adventures from previous years. By now, some students have begun to ask about their own inquiry conference. *Will there be one? Do we get to go?*

New to the classroom by midyear are a variety of student contracts that permit the children to pursue more in-depth investigations than those experienced in the relatively short discovery periods. (See Appendices U and V, pages 158 and 159, for a sample science inquiry contract and inquiry investigation plan.) With a contract, a student who has become intrigued by a particular topic can branch off and investigate a question in far more detail. The contracts clearly define expectations. The teacher provides class time in return for a promise by the student to complete the provisions defined in the contract. Students are rewarded by being exempt from selected class work. The contracts are accompanied by contract journals in which students document exactly what they have done and what the results have been. These contract journals will be invaluable later as students consider presenting their findings at KIC.

Also by midyear, we have established the Science Review Board. The SRB is a committee of three students who have several responsibilities. Entries for the *Book of Student Discoveries* must first be approved by the SRB. The board doesn't consider the validity of the discovery; that is for future students to decide based upon the credibility of the entry and any replications that may follow. Rather, the SRB determines if sufficient details are included so that the discovery *can* be repeated. Since the page in the *Book of Student Discoveries* will be read by students in future years, it is vital that the entry be clear and complete with the necessary steps, measurements, and procedures for replication to occur. Once the SRB decides the entry is acceptable, the page is stamped and officially placed into the discovery book.

Other duties of the SRB include assistance with the discovery boxes. They take inventories for replenishment of consumables, check boxes after use to ensure proper cleanup, and maintain the science materials in the classroom. The more responsibility and ownership the kids assume, the more time the classroom teacher can devote to other matters.

At this point in the year I have invited the class to apply for *PTA inquiry grants*. (A sample inquiry grant proposal is included in Appendix I, pages 144–145.) Money is available from the PTA to purchase materials for inquiry investigations that may not be available in the classroom. A variety of catalogs are available in the classroom for students to find needed materials. (A list of science catalogs is included in Chapter 11.) Grants of ten or fifteen dollars are awarded based upon the grant proposals. The SRB assists with review of proposals and helps decide if grants are warranted. As the students seek sources for funding, they come to understand another aspect of being a scientist: finding money to continue their research. It seems there is so much more to science than merely science.

It is shortly after the winter holiday that I introduce the KIC website *(esiponline.learnserver.net/kic)* to the class along with the possibility of actually attending the conference. The website (described in detail in Chapter 11) makes the upcoming conference even more real for the students. As we begin to talk about KIC, the website is available to describe the conference, provide copies of past KIC articles, and let kids communicate with KIC students from the past.

To introduce the conference and to answer some common questions asked each year, I distribute the *KIC Is Coming* information sheet. (A sample is included in Appendix K, page 147.) This helps both students and parents begin to understand what KIC is and how our class will prepare for the conference.

And then the KIC applications arrive. For the kids, it all becomes suddenly real. Sometimes the kids worry that they have nothing worthwhile to contribute to the conference. I remind them of the many questions they have been asking, their experiences with the discovery boxes, and their documentation on the discovery box log pages, and I point to the many entries made into the book of discoveries. Those students working with contracts have already been gathering new data and plan to continue their investigations in a variety of ways. By now, the students consider themselves scientists doing the things that scientists do. I remind them that scientists go to conferences and tell of their ongoing investigations. There are stories to tell and there are other students who want to hear those stories. KIC is the ideal place to share with the world what has been going on in the classroom. The process of filling out the applications begins.

There are two different applications for KIC: one to present and one to provide a hands-on activity. (Sample application forms are included in Appendices A and B, pages 134 and 136.) The application to present asks the students to describe their original question, explain the investigation being conducted to answer it, list the materials being used, and explain how the students plan to convince their audience that their findings are accurate. The role of the classroom teacher becomes that of coach, helping the students with the authentic activity of completing an application. "Someone far away will read the application," I tell the students, "and you want to make sure that you convince them that your research is worthy of a place at the conference." The stress level begins to rise.

Hands-on activities at the conference provide opportunities for visitors to actually manipulate materials. The application to provide such activities asks the students to describe what their visitors will do, what materials will be used, and what they hope visitors will learn. A table is reserved for each student or group of students accepted to provide the activities. Students prepare written directions, guest registers, and handouts as part of the activity.

By late February, the applications are due and sent to the KIC Committee. As the investigations continue, the students eagerly await responses.

The KIC Committee

Imagine the year is 1947. Everything is in black and white. Within a large city building several floors above the noisy street, a smoke-filled conference room is crowded with education officials from around the state. The long table in the middle of the room is overflowing with binders and folders amid stacks of applications being noisily reviewed by clusters of educators. The papers are being passed around, vigorously debated, and separated into various piles based upon hard-negotiated decisions. Suddenly, the doors burst open with deliveries of more applications yet to be reviewed. A fresh supply of coffee and doughnuts has arrived at last and is being passed around the table. It has been a long evening and there is much to be done before the meeting will end.

When I imagine a KIC Committee meeting, this is what I see. At least that is how it might look in the movies. And when I talk about the distant, mysterious KIC Committee with the class, I smile at the sight of that image in my mind. Of course it, and the KIC Committee itself, is pure fiction. And I don't describe the committee to the students in quite those terms.

So if there is no KIC Committee, no noisy smoke-filled room full of educators from distant places, where do the applications go when they are sent off, and who decides if those applications are accepted or not? The KIC Committee resides in the mind of the classroom teacher; indeed the committee *is* the classroom teacher. The teacher sets the deadlines, encourages excellence, responds to applications that need revision or added detail, and blames it all on the committee. The reader is now privy to one of the best-kept secrets of the past decade. Like Santa Claus or the tooth fairy, the KIC Committee is a grand pretense—wonderful yet imaginary.

Throughout the process of preparing for the conference, my role as the classroom teacher is that of coach. I want my kids to do their best as they conceptualize their ideas on the applications. They are writing to persuade someone far away that they are worthy of being considered for a conference. By the time spring arrives, I am more like their parent than a teacher. So, I speak of someone other than myself who will review what the kids write. It really does heighten the drama and I suppose the level of stress, but I am convinced it also raises the quality of the applications and the serious manner in which the students approach the conference.

continued

Some teachers *do* get together and review the applications for one another or have students in other classes assess the completed applications. This process can sometimes be lengthy. The important thing is that the students get timely feedback and it is usually most efficient for each teacher to process her or his own students' applications. Time must then be allotted for writing the response letters back to the kids. This is best done by someone who really knows the students.

Virtually all applications are accepted. On those rare occasions when an application is not quite satisfactory because of flawed methods (in spite of all the assistance offered in the classroom) or a lack of details, or if safety issues are a concern, a letter from the committee is far easier for kids to accept than comments from the teacher. The students and teacher can then work together to respond to the letter, hoping to address the problem as a team. If the student should choose not to respond or if the response is not adequate, it is the committee and not the teacher making that final decision.

Some might think it inauthentic to have a pretend committee play such an important role in the months leading up to the conference. In fact, the role of any adult other than the classroom teacher or the parent should *not* be crucial to the success of the child. The true motivation to participate in the conference and do one's best should be something other than a desire to please an adult. That's not what scientists do. The ultimate goal for each child is to attend the conference and convince his or her peers that his or her data are accurate and discoveries valid. Being accepted and deemed credible by one's colleagues is far more powerful than a grade or a ribbon decided upon by an adult. The concept of a KIC Committee is just enough spice to make the stew a bit more exciting.

Spring

It was mid-March and the students were eagerly anticipating the responses from the KIC Committee. They knew that any day a call would come from the office announcing the delivery of that special package. Today was that day.

"Mr. Pearce," the office secretary said from the speaker in the ceiling, "you have a large envelope here in the office."

The excitement among the students was difficult to contain. Our class courier immediately went to the office to pick up the package.

The students seemed rather nervous as they awaited her return. Having told of their investigations and discoveries on the applications weeks before, the children were eager to have the chance to go to the conference and share with other kids all that they had done. Finally the time had come to find out what the KIC Committee thought of their ideas.

The courier returned with the large package. Inside were individual envelopes addressed to each student who had applied to present or provide a hands-on activity. (A sample acceptance letter is included in Appendix H, page 143.) I read their names and handed out the envelopes. Quietly, the students opened them.

Within seconds there was screaming and jumping.

"What did they say?" I asked. "Are you in?"

"They accepted my proposal!" shouted one student.

"I have a table reserved for my hands-on," another announced.

"They really liked our ideas," others said. "They want us to do our presentation!"

Amid all the excitement, there suddenly settled in a sobering realization. Imagine being a third- or fourth- or fifth-grade student and finding out that you will be doing a presentation in front of strangers at a real science conference far away from your school. These young scientists, who had done so many things that scientists do, were about to do perhaps the toughest thing of all: try to convince their peers that the science they had done was valid and accurate. My challenge in the coming weeks was to instill a sense of confidence in each student. KIC was coming, our class was going, and many of us had been selected to contribute. It just doesn't get any more authentic than that!

After being accepted to present at KIC, the students begin writing their articles for the *KIC Journal*. (Guidelines for writing the KIC article are included in Appendix J, page 146.) We go back to past journals and review the articles written by former students. Which were really convincing and interesting and what did the authors include to make them so? Which ones were too shallow, with only partial data or sketchy details? As the kids evaluate the writing of others, they are able to assess the quality of their own writing.

As the weeks move closer to the conference a variety of communications take place among the classes who plan to attend. Students prepare for the conference and gain a sense of shared interest and community writing letters and emails, sharing videos of themselves describing their investigations, using the KIC website, and asking questions about one another's topics. Additionally, the KIC Committee sends several letters and reminders to the presenters, offering encouragement and guidelines for a quality presentation. The classroom teacher has been gathering data with weekly KIC progress reports, which help assess student progress and possible problems. (A sample progress report is located in Appendix S, page 155.)

With merely weeks to go, I asked presenters to prepare blurbs for their presentations—two- or three-sentence descriptions to be used for student sign-ups. Along with the blurbs and a schedule for the day, each classroom teacher receives sign-up sheets for students to use to decide how to schedule their day at KIC. Usually, there are three sessions of about forty-five minutes each. During each session, presentations are going on concurrently in numerous rooms, with three or four presentations completed per room per session. The sign-up sheets indicate which presentations will be scheduled for which rooms. Students sign up for the presentations they'd like to attend before the conference, and spots are limited, so that each room is evenly attended. I also asked students to prepare biographical sketches that moderators will use to introduce students in each session. (A sample biographical sketch sheet and guidelines for writing blurbs are included in Appendices C and P, pages 138 and 152.)

One Week Before KIC

Each week the kids have been completing the KIC progress reports. At the end of each report is a scale for the students to self-assess their stress level. Not only is it interesting to see how the kids are feeling as the conference approaches (their stress levels do noticeably increase), but it is also important for the students to maintain focus and not have the date of the conference catch them by surprise. The stress level also rises for the teacher. There have been years when I thought we would never be ready. Yet I have never been disappointed by the performance of the students. They always seem to come through.

The week before the conference is a busy one. Students must sign up for presentation sessions. They practice giving presentations to one another in the classroom and in neighboring classes. This is especially important for younger grades since these practice presentations are great models for next year's students. Overheads and handouts are prepared. Students providing hands-on activities show samples to classmates. Checklists are developed so nothing is forgotten on the day of the conference. (A set of sample guidelines for KIC presentations is provided in Appendix R, page 154.)

Then suddenly, the day of KIC has arrived.

The Big Day

The bus ride to the conference is an interesting one. The bus is loaded with boxes of materials and charts. Throughout the ride, students are looking over note cards and working together on last-minute preparations.

I, too, am a bit anxious. Because of its authenticity, KIC may seem a bit unpredictable. *Will my students do the best they can? Will they convince the other children of their discoveries? How will everyone behave? Will the visitors be as impressed as I have been these last several weeks?* These and other questions and doubts go through every teacher's mind.

Soon we arrive. The students are wearing their color-coded name tags, which remind them of the rooms for which they signed up. In we go to the large meeting area to be greeted and welcomed and then dismissed to the presentation rooms. The weeks and months of planning, going back to that day so long ago when the students first arrived, have brought us here. And as my students begin their presentations, I heave a sigh of relief. Another year of real science has brought us to KIC.

Suddenly, KIC Is Over

When the day has ended, we gather all the things we brought to the conference. Those kids who provided hands-on activities clean up their areas and look over the guest registers. Those who did presentations are satisfied that they truly did their best. They are excited that their audience was actually interested and asked questions. On the bus, we quietly browse through the new *KIC Journals*, looking for names and articles we recognize. The authors know that future students will read about what happened at KIC today.

That evening there are stories to be told around the dinner table; stories of a day that these young scientists will never forget.

In the days that remain before summer, we talk about what happened at the conference and where the kids will go from here. There are those who will continue their research, spurred on by the questions and discussions at the conference. For them, KIC was not a destination but rather a stopping point along the trail of scientific inquiry.

Everyone completes the postconference surveys (see samples in Appendices N and O, pages 150 and 151) and relives the year of discovery we have shared. The students have entered the culture of a classroom that is not only a community for one particular year but one that continues to grow as new students come and read and learn about the past and, most importantly, look to the future.

> *The important thing is not to stop questioning.*
>
> Albert Einstein

References

Pearce, Charles. 1999. *Nurturing Inquiry: Real Science for the Elementary Classroom*. Portsmouth, NH: Heinemann.

4 KIC in the Classroom, Part 1: Laying the Foundation Through Exploration

As Charlie's classroom story illustrates, planning for KIC really begins on day one as the seeds of inquiry are planted. Those seeds are nurtured through the early months of the school year as students explore the world around them and begin to craft questions that will lead them from open-ended exploration to focused investigation as the year progresses. The following are some frequently asked questions concerning how to get started with inquiry.

What are some ways to foster inquiry in the classroom early in the school year?

Read-Alouds and Think-Alouds

By modeling curiosity and question posing, a teacher can offer students new ways of approaching a book and problematizing seemingly static information. The more explicit the teacher can be about his thinking processes, the better: "When I look at this picture of children playing in the wind, I think of the wind near our school. It always seems strongest to me over near Ms. Foster's room," or "I wonder what the author means when she says . . . ," or "Wait, this seems different than what I read in book X. I wonder how to decide which author to believe."

Donna Dieckman reads books about scientists and their work to inspire questions. Books such as *A Snake Scientist* and *Elephant Woman* invite students into the field with working scientists to explore their questions and the challenges scientists encounter in their work. Books such as *Echoes for the Eye: Poems to Celebrate Patterns in Nature* and *How to Be a Nature Detective* inspire students to develop more sophisticated observation skills and think more closely about the processes of science. (See Chapter 11 for more information on these and other engaging science books.) Books such as these also provide context-specific and often creative problem-solving approaches to science that may support students in their own scientific investigations.

See Chapter 6 for additional ideas about using science-related read-alouds and think-alouds.

The Outdoor Classroom

An often unused and valuable resource awaits teachers and students right outside their classrooms. The school yard is an amazing science laboratory and provides opportunities for close observations and explorations that foster questions and further investigations in the classroom. Whether you have them observe shadows on the blacktop at various times in the day, document the changes to the trees and flowers as the seasons change, place thermometers in various locations outside to note temperature variations, or analyze the construction of playground equipment, providing time for students to become more familiar with their surroundings undoubtedly sparks questions.

> Early in the school year, provide students with a magnifying glass and a 3-foot piece of yarn to mark off a small circle of the school yard of interest to them. Invite students to observe that area up close, noting their observations, surprises, and questions in their scientist notebooks.

Open-Ended Inquiry Periods

Charles Pearce introduces students to inquiry early in the year by providing opportunities for students to explore a variety of guided hands-on science activities stationed around the classroom. According to Charlie, "Each is designed to elicit lots of questions, tap prior knowledge, and intrigue students with both new and more familiar topics and activities. This inquiry period is an early start toward a more independent student-directed inquiry process to follow later." (Read more about Charlie's approach in Chapter 3.)

Beginning-of-the-year inquiry periods can also be used to introduce students to the exploration of interesting materials. Jeanne Reardon's class began exploring water drops after observing raindrops on the windows and windowsills. Using eye droppers and materials for different surfaces, students generated many observations and questions about the movement of water. A poorly performing marker in another classroom was a catalyst for an exploration of various brands of markers. Students compared markers by designing various tests and then evaluating the markers in terms of performance and cost. As students explore various materials, they are introduced to tools of inquiry, such as magnifying glasses, timers, and measuring devices. Time spent early in the year becoming familiar with various materials and tools will support students as they develop more focused investigations later.

Scientist Visits

Fourth-grade teacher Maureen Hoyer invited practicing scientists into her classroom early in the year to introduce her students to their work. These visiting scientists also introduced students to diverse and interesting fields of study, such as polymers.

Donna Dieckman organized a Science Awareness Week at her elementary school to welcome scientists from the community to share their work with students. Many of the scientists brought artifacts of their work to share as well as hands-on materials and activities to engage students in their field of study. Students interacted with chemists, biologists, astrophysicists, geologists, archaeologists, and botanists, and they were introduced to a variety of scientific fields of study. Many of these scientists continued to serve as scientists on call so that students could contact them with questions throughout the school year.

Jeanne Reardon introduced students to science in the field by taking them on field trips to a hardware store and a lumberyard. Students learned about a variety of materials and gained a sense of how science is used every day in a variety of settings.

How can I help students recognize and ask more probing questions?

Jeanne Reardon states that the essence of inquiry is providing opportunities for students to explore authentic questions and problems that emanate from their own experiences, curiosities, and interests. It is through these opportunities that students begin to develop the "behaviors of inquiry—asking questions, looking for answers to questions, observing change, building explanations based on observation, making connections between what they already know and new observations, [and] planning investigations to understand 'strange things.'"

Though student questions may be the heart of inquiry, it takes time for quality questions to emerge. What do we mean by *quality questions*? Quality questions are generative questions. They are designed to lead somewhere—to have "legs." They are questions that inspire wonder and provide opportunities for deeper investigation and critical thinking. Such questions emerge from students' experiences and opportunities for exploration of the world around them. They emerge from conversations between friends. They emerge from reading and listening to books that inspire wonder. They emerge from immersion in a topic of study that provides time for students to explore and investigate. Through such opportunities, students begin to notice things that surprise them and they begin to wonder. They begin to ask questions that are rooted in their need to know more and understand better.

Teachers can also encourage student questioning by asking questions that support critical thinking:

- What did you notice?
- Why do you think that . . . ?
- What surprised you while you were . . . ?
- What are you thinking about . . . now?
- What seemed to work well?
- When there was a problem, what did you do?
- What new questions do you have?
- What are your plans for further investigation?

What are some of the things I need to consider when planning for inquiry?

As you consider how to incorporate inquiry into your classroom, you may want to think about the following:

- *Time:* Inquiry takes time. Can you organize larger blocks for inquiry? Will students have regular time periods throughout the year to continue their work?
- *Materials:* What materials are available to you and your students? How will you organize materials? Are there places designated for students to store their materials for ongoing investigations?
- *Procedures:* How will materials be distributed and collected? Where will students work? How will students share their findings?
- *Record keeping:* How will students record their data, reflections, and questions? How will you document observation and planning notes?

What are some effective models for classroom inquiry?

There are two models that have proved successful for teachers of a variety of classes. Each model is based on the principles of exploration, cooperation, and collaboration. These are not blueprints that must be followed to the letter, but guides intended to help you design the structure that will work best for your students.

Model One: Science Workshop

You can read more about Jeanne Reardon's version of a science workshop in greater detail in *Science Workshop* (Saul et al. 2002) but the following is the basic organization of a science workshop.

- *Class meeting with minilessons* (10–15 minutes). Instruction focuses on developing (1) a skill the teacher anticipates the students will need in the day's investigation or (2) a previously taught skill that needs revisiting and refinement. At the end of the meeting the teacher reads down the class list, recalling each student's plan for the investigation period. Possible topics for minilessons include:
    - procedures (safety rules, using materials, journal writing, getting help)
    - tools (demonstrating how to use hand lens, balance, measurement tools)
    - problems (thinking about specific problems and possible approaches)
    - process (modeling conventions used by scientists as they work: observation, record keeping, organizing and analyzing data, replication, variables)
    - science writing and record keeping (modeling scientist's notebook writing, scientific drawings, labels, charts, coding journal entries)
    - reading and using science trade books and other resources (finding information, taking notes, evaluating credibility of resources)
    - plans (discussing and writing about what to do next)
- *Exploration and investigation; writing and record keeping* (approximately 45 minutes). Students work independently or in small groups on their own inquiries. Students make entries in their scientist's notebooks, recording observations, questions, data, and so forth as they explore and investigate. (See additional information about scientist's notebooks in Chapter 6.) The teacher focuses and supports inquiries by listening, questioning, identifying needs, assessing progress, and selecting skills to teach during future minilessons. Students use the last ten minutes to reflect on the day's work and record plans for the next workshop.
- *Scientists' meeting* (30–40 minutes). This meeting provides time for students to present their work, try out their ideas in front of their own community of scientists, receive feedback, and respond to their peers' questions. A few students may report findings from their investigations, request ideas for data analysis or addressing a problem they are struggling with, or demonstrate a procedure they are using. The teacher facilitates discussion, encourages participation, and records students' questions on a chart. At the end of the scientists' meeting, the teacher records each student's plans for the next workshop.

Model Two: Inquiry Period

Charles Pearce uses fifty-minute blocks of inquiry time and pre- and postactivities that occur several times during a month in his classroom. Charlie introduces the inquiry period using open-ended inquiry activities and then moves to the use of discovery boxes. Later in the year, students use the inquiry period for more self-directed inquiry investigations. Charlie describes his approach as a highway where students see interesting side roads. The teacher plans the "highway activities" but encourages side trips through discussion and student contracts and by having materials for exploration available.

- *Preinquiry procedures* (varying amounts of time). Prior to a scheduled inquiry period, the teacher plans an investigation or has students (in groups of two or three) sign up for a box of materials they plan to explore. Students check the materials list, request any additional materials they'll need, and submit an initial plan for the inquiry period. They also have access to the trade books and discovery log entries to do some background reading on their topic.

- *Investigation and documentation time* (50 minutes). During the inquiry period, students use the materials to investigate their question(s). They record their data on a discovery log form, which becomes part of the log record in the discovery box. They may also record thoughts and ideas in a dialogue journal or submit an entry to the *Book of Student Discoveries*. The teacher visits with groups of students, asks questions, and participates in discussions as students are conducting their investigations.

- *Debriefing* (approximately 30 minutes). After the inquiry period, students report back to the class. They share information about their boxes, their investigations, and their discoveries. This unpacking is essential because it affords students the opportunity to make public their questions and findings and inspires new questions and curiosities.

However you decide to organize inquiry time, key elements include time for focused minilessons and preparation, exploration and investigation, and community meeting and discussion.

Inquiry does not need to be confined into a science period. There is a literacy connection (note taking, documentation, research, communication, composition), a math connection (measuring, graphing, calculating), and even an art connection (diagramming, sketching, labeling). Essentially, an inquiry period can be justified for almost every subject of the day.

My school has very few science materials. Where can I find materials?

It's amazing how much science can be done with very common, everyday materials, such as cotton balls, toothpicks, and string. (A list of the most common materials used for investigations is located in Chapter 11.)

Here are a few ideas for acquiring materials:

- Check out some of the storage closets in your school. It's amazing how many materials can be mined from old science kits and other resource kits that have long been forgotten.
- Include a notice in the school or class newsletter periodically with a list of materials students will be using. It's a great way to find out which parents have connections to the toothpick factory across town!
- Send a letter to major companies in the area requesting donations of materials—for instance, many film developing centers discard empty film canisters, which are ideal for floating, storing, and rocket construction!
- Grant funding is often available; check with your administrator for a list of local grants and check online for regional and national grants.
- Visit local grocery stores and other neighborhood businesses to request donations personally. Don't forget to mention that donations to public schools are tax deductible!

What are some other resources that support inquiry?

Check out Chapter 11 for more information on literature- and Web-based resources as well as human resources that support inquiry.

References

Saul, W., et al. 2002. *Science Workshop: Reading, Writing and Thinking Like a Scientist*. Portsmouth, NH: Heinemann.

5 KIC in the Classroom, Part 2: Moving Beyond Exploration to Investigation and Presentation

Many teachers don't even mention KIC to students until midyear. By then, students have been immersed in inquiry explorations and investigations that have laid a foundation for the more focused investigations that will lead to presentations at KIC. Teachers also have had time to establish routines and work out logistical issues that will support continued inquiry through the year. The following are frequently asked questions related to participating in KIC and supporting KIC in the classroom.

How can I introduce KIC to students?

Although we all have the vision of the absentminded professor who works in an isolated lab, the truth is that scientists isolate themselves only until they have something to share. The opportunity to share questions and discoveries is a natural evolution and an important part of inquiry. Just as scientists share their work with their colleagues, KIC provides an opportunity for young scientists to share their work with peers. It also provides a catalyst to help students move from exploration to more focused investigations and analysis.

When introducing KIC, it is important to present the conference in such a way that students do not view it as a final step, but rather an opportunity to share their work in progress. As teacher Deb Galinski reflects, "I do not want that 'science fair' thing hanging over their heads." Just as an investigation begins with a question, KIC presentations almost always end with "My question now is . . ."

Through the years teachers have introduced KIC to students in a variety of ways, helping them gain some sense of what the conference is all about. The following are a few examples:

- Visit the KIC website *(esiponline.learnserver.net/kic)* and show students the KIC slide show. Ask students what they notice and discuss it as a class.

- Provide students with an invitation letter to announce that KIC is coming. (A sample is provided in Appendix K.)
- Share prior *KIC Journals* with students and discuss the journal articles.
- Invite KIC alumni to visit the class and share their experiences with students and field initial questions.
- Show a KIC video from a previous KIC and discuss student observations and questions.
- Share information about professional scientist meetings and conferences and discuss the opportunity for students to participate in a similar conference through KIC.

Once students have some sense about what KIC is all about, the work of deciding what to investigate begins.

What is the appropriate role for parents before and during the inquiry conference?

The assistance of parents on the day of the conference is crucial. Parents help transport materials, assist with setup and cleanup, direct students between sessions, and generally serve as additional eyes and ears for the teachers. However, guidelines must be established well before the conference to prevent parents from infringing on the student-centered nature of the day. Conducting parent information night early in the planning process and sending home several memos help alleviate potential problems.

The overall role of parents must be a minor one. We consider authentic student questions as the driving force in the inquiry process; parents who interfere by bringing their own adult values and prejudices to the project do a disservice to the children they are trying to help.

Parents are interesting and as varied as the children we teach. Think of parents as falling anywhere along a spectrum. At one end are those who insist on doing everything and being part of every project and assignment. Nothing the child does on his own is quite good enough and the parent feels compelled to constantly step in and fix any problems. Sometimes these parents become so absorbed in the project that they completely take over its direction and outcome.

On the opposite end of the spectrum are the parents who take a completely hands-off approach. Perhaps because of disinterest, an overly busy schedule, or a belief that the child must sink or swim on her own, these parents offer little assistance.

To be honest, children who are engaged in their own investigations based upon questions they developed themselves will need little, if any, parental support. The child is driven to find out for herself. She does not want to be told the answers or shown the results by someone else. Parents can provide guidance, especially when difficulties arise, but only when the child seeks out that assistance. On the day of the conference the student will be open to the questions and scrutiny of other scientists. She must be the expert as she explains and participates in a discussion about her investigation.

Appendix M (see page 149) is a sample parent memo about appropriate parental roles when working with young scientists both at home and at the conference.

Where do KIC questions come from?

Students have already spent several months exploring materials, their environment, and the curriculum, so they may already have a good sense of what they would like to focus on for KIC. Perhaps there is a topic they keep returning to that just fascinates them or something new and exciting that they've only recently discovered. For other students, it's very difficult. Perhaps they are dabblers who are interested in just about everything, or perhaps they just haven't found something that has sparked their interest.

KIC ideas have come from just about everywhere. As Maureen Hoyer sums up, questions come from "old science units, personal interest questions, family interests, demonstrations seen (either from a real scientist or on television), or something students have read." Jenny Zmarzly adds that everyday events can also be a wonderful source. One of her students' projects was inspired by a stop at the school water fountain and a discussion about how it worked. Revisit some of the question engines from Charlie's class story (see Chapter 3) and the discussion about questions at the beginning of this chapter for more ideas on sparking questions in the classroom.

As important as questions are, it's important to allow them to incubate over time and grow and change as students focus in on what they really want to investigate. Settling too quickly on a definitive question can sometimes lead to roadblocks. Maureen Hoyer asks her students to think about a topic or question over winter break and then allows students to explore the question during January to refine their choices. As students bounce ideas off each other, what they want to do begins to take shape. Questions continue to change over the course of the investigations and this journey is an all-important part of the inquiry process.

Given curricular and time constraints, it may be tempting to confine student questions within certain boundaries. Susan Wells recalls that during her first year with KIC, her class was participating in the JASON Project with National Geographic, which focuses on tube worms, gray whales, and underwater exploration. She thought it would be a good idea for students to focus their topics around this project. One group, however, was quite determined that it wanted to investigate solar ovens, even though the students had to do their investigation outside of class. At KIC, they demonstrated that they really owned their project and were very proud to share what they had discovered. Susan admits, "This little group taught me that when given freedom, these ten-year-old scientists would develop their own questions based on interest . . . there was no need for teacher-induced motivation. Their question was all the motivation they needed . . . I never tried to control my kids' topics again."

Sampling of Where KIC Questions Come From

- A project on the lasting effects of gum flavor came from a discussion between two students about which brand of spearmint gum had the longest-lasting flavor.

- An investigation of structural design and weight developed when a student watched a television show on structures.

- A visit to caverns in the Shenandoah Valley sparked an interest in learning more about natural crystals.

- Plans to plant a garden at an urban school raised the question of how to keep pests, particularly rats, out of the garden, which became the basis for an investigation.

- The seeds for an investigation of the weather's effect on plants developed from a third-grade unit on plant growth and development.

- A school visit by a scientist inspired an investigation of common kitchen chemicals.

How are KIC groups formed?

As students try on questions and topics, it's natural that they will discover other students with similar interests. This is the birthplace of KIC groups. As opposed to forming groups according to academic strengths and weaknesses, gender, personalities, or other criteria, this is an opportunity to allow groups to form by interest and a desire to work together. Of course, that does not guarantee that all groups will work out as planned. As with questions, allowing groups to be flexible and establishing protocols for settling disputes greatly enhances the success of the experience. Deb Galinski also recommends that students be allowed to work alone if they so choose.

Similarly, most teachers recommend that students be allowed to define their own roles within their groups. Teachers can provide opportunities for class discussions that facilitate informed decisions. This allows opportunities for leaders to emerge and for students to discover their own strengths and weaknesses within a group. As Betty Lobe states, "Students need to be given permission to do their own decision making."

How can I fit inquiry and the planning for an inquiry conference into an already busy day?

Inquiry science in the classroom addresses far more than just science. The activities and behaviors exhibited by kids who are involved in their own science beg the question How can we *not* include inquiry for our students? A story from Charlie Pearce's classroom illustrates the point.

> One morning before the start of school, a student asked if later that day we were going to be doing "school science" or "real science." I wasn't sure what he meant until he explained.
>
> "School science," he said, "is when we all do the same things together and follow the teacher's directions."
>
> "Real science," he went on, "is when we get the chance to do our own explorations."
>
> We were doing both. The school science in our classroom addressed the traditional, content-oriented science curriculum. The real science provided a means to extend and enrich what was already started.

When our students set out on their own investigations, they are using what they have already learned to discover new things. Benjamin Bloom identified this as application and synthesis on his taxonomy of thinking. Inquiry science, the "real" science in our classrooms, enhances higher levels of thinking. Time in the day other than that reserved for traditional science is well spent in these endeavors.

Adult scientists communicate extensively. They read to find what is already known and to see what others have been doing, and they write to record their own investigations and discoveries. As kids are given opportunities to engage in authentic science, they too are drawn into the genuine needs to communicate. What better time in the school day to address these needs than during language arts time? For many teachers, inquiry science activities are actually prewriting activities because of the writing opportunities they provide. There is no reason that science cannot be exploited to enhance our students' desire to read and write.

As students prepare for KIC, they must plan their presentations. They must display data and communicate about it in ways that are accurate and credible. They plan handouts, prepare and organize overheads and note cards, and practice the actual presentations in front of the class prior to the conference. In addition, they must write and revise *KIC Journal* articles as well as research background information to tell what others have already discovered. These may be things adult scientists do as they plan for their own conferences, but much of these planning activities are, in reality, related to language arts. I have had no difficulty justifying my use of language arts time to engage in inquiry science and to plan for the inquiry conference. By doing so, I am able to squeeze so much more into each school day.

What are some practical ideas for managing KIC materials in the classroom?

- Have students brainstorm a list of materials they anticipate needing. Send home a letter to parents asking for donations of any of the materials needed. (See the list of most common materials needed in Chapter 11.)

- Place a notice in the school newsletter or PTA newsletter asking for needed materials. Place a collection box outside your classroom door or near the office for easy drop-off of materials.

- Solicit local businesses for donations.

- Charlie Pearce asks the PTA for a small amount of funds to support KIC and invites his students to write a grant proposal based on their project to get funding support (see Appendix I, page 144, for a sample grant form).

- Designate a storage box for each group to use to keep its materials and ongoing work in so that the group can easily access it as needed and transport it as needed.

What other resources are helpful to support students?

- Review the general science websites and ask-an-expert websites in Chapter 11 and bookmark ones that are appropriate for your students on your computers so that students can gain easy access to sites that have been screened for appropriateness.

- Collaborate with your school's media specialist to develop some minilessons on research-related and informational book browsing to support students with their research. Provide the media specialist with a list of topics students are investigating so he can gather appropriate science trade books for students to have as resources.

- Human resources can be invaluable to young scientists. Some possibilities include KIC alumni, high school and college students, local business community members, and inquiry pen pals (from other classes or schools participating in KIC). Of course, the best human resources are the experts within your own class. It's amazing what students bring with them to the classroom that may be quite helpful to someone else.

How do students apply to present at KIC?

After students have had some time to explore their topics and form their groups, it is time for them to apply to present at KIC. Students may choose to do either a presentation or a hands-on demonstration (depending upon what choices are available; see "Deciding What Elements of KIC to Include" in Chapter 10 for more details). Sample applications are available in Appendices A and B, pages 134 and 136.

This is an authentic opportunity for literacy-related minilessons about informational writing and the real-life task of completing forms neatly and accurately. It is also an opportunity to engage students in peer conferencing and editing, during which they can provide each other with constructive feedback regarding their applications.

Once applications are completed, they are "sent" to the KIC Committee for review. As Charles Pearce explained in Chapter 3, the KIC Committee is often the classroom teacher incognito. However, the KIC Committee can also be a consortium of teachers and/or school personnel or include members of the outside community. The purpose is simply to review the applications and provide any important feedback that might help students with their projects.

Students then usually receive an acceptance letter with guidelines for their KIC presentation (see sample in Appendix H, page 143.)

What are some of the common challenges that occur?

As students continue their investigations, challenges are bound to arise. These too present an opportunity for students to learn and practice problem-solving skills. Students who are engaged in inquiry investigations eventually learn to view setbacks as opportunities for further investigation rather than as failures. Following are some common situations that may occur:

Experiment Failures

Students can be disappointed when they have worked diligently to set up an experiment and the results are unexpected or the materials do not work properly. They may even become so discouraged that they want to stop their investigation for fear that they will have nothing to share at KIC.

Be prepared to share with students some books about scientists and their experiences with the unexpected. (A list of books about scientists and their work is provided in Chapter 11.) For example, in the book *Snowflake Bentley* (Martin 1998), farmer and scientist Wilson Bentley took more than six thousand photographs before he successfully captured his first complete snowflake on film. Providing examples of how important failure is to science will help young scientists continue their work.

A wonderful KIC example occurred several years ago. A group of four young scientists investigated how to grow plants in an urban garden. They were trying to determine the optimal conditions for different seeds given the environmental conditions that existed. After three months of investigation, not a single one of their plants was a success. They turned failure into success, though. They learned something new about plants with each failure, so instead of bringing a bevy of plants to show off at KIC, they brought a chart of ten things they learned not to do in order to grow plants successfully.

Changing Questions

As discussed previously, this can be a good thing, especially if the question is evolving based on the investigative process. This can also be viewed positively if the initial question is leading to a dead end or students lose interest in it very quickly. But it can also be frustrating, especially when students are really on to something and they decide to turn in a different direction. However, if students are to succeed at planning and evaluating their own work, they have to be allowed to make some wrong turns.

Changing Groups

This too can be positive or negative, depending on the specifics. As Maureen Hoyer says, "Sometimes two can be too large of a group." If the dynamics of the group are impeding the work and conflict resolution strategies have been unsuccessful, it may be better to let the group disband and reform in another configuration. Sometimes a large group splits into two smaller groups so that each can focus on a more specific aspect of a topic. Sometimes individual students decide to team up and combine their efforts. Betty Lobe suggests that teachers treat the grouping as their own personal inquiry. "Observe what works and why. Learn from them."

Lack of Resources

There is perhaps nothing more frustrating than having a desire to do something but a lack of materials to do it with. Obviously there are limits. Students may want to have a car engine to take apart, but that just may not be possible to achieve. But given that most materials students need for investigations are pretty common, this can be an opportunity to become very resourceful. Even difficult materials are not impossible to obtain.

Finding Materials

Treasures from Trash

It's amazing what you can do with "trash." A few years back, one class managed to get almost all its needed materials by soliciting items that are commonly thrown away. Empty coffee cans became experimental watering tubes. Disposable muffin tins became seed-germinating cups. Empty thread spools became experimental wheels and pulleys.

The Bold and the Brave

A group that wanted to investigate polymers wrote to a company that produced polymer materials and asked for a sample. The company was so interested in the student research that it sent the students enough materials to conduct investigations for the rest of the year.

What do students need to do to prepare their investigations for presentation?

About six weeks before KIC, most teachers begin helping students transition from active investigation to preparing for their presentations. This is a time for students to reflect on their journey so far, complete any experiments in progress, wrap up their research, and begin to review their data, notes, and materials. As they analyze and synthesize their data, students begin to craft the stories they want to tell.

Titles and Blurbs

A first step in this transition is for students to decide on names for their presentations and compose short blurbs that will be used to advertise their sessions to other KIC attendees. This is an opportunity to practice persuasive writing—all scientists want a full house when they unveil their discoveries! A blurb preparation sheet is provided in Appendix P, page 152.

Journal Articles

As they review and organize their data, students need to begin to think about what to include in their journal articles, which will be published records of their investigations. A journal article guideline sheet is provided in Appendix J, page 146. The *KIC Journal* includes articles for all presentations so that students can read about everyone's work, especially those presentations they are unable to attend. The *KIC Journal*s have become not only a source of information but also an inspiration to future KIC participants who read about the work of those who came before them.

The *KIC Journal* article provides an authentic purpose for teaching writing craft minilessons related to information alwriting. Minilessons such as how to weave data charts into text, how to use descriptive detail, and how to use subheadings effectively are invaluable because students have a need to know these skills and can apply them readily to their writing.

Presentations

In addition to preparing journal articles, students are planning their presentations. A presentation guideline sheet is included in Appendix R, page 154. Most presentations are about seven to ten minutes in length, so students need to decide what to include, what to leave out, and how best to tell the story they want to tell. This is also a great opportunity to teach minilessons on effective communication skills and preparation of presentation materials, including the application of technology; students have incorporated PowerPoint and video clips in previous KIC presentations.

Once students have prepared their presentations, the all-important rehearsal for the big day begins. Students should be able to say their presentations, not read them off cards or a script. Since they will be fielding questions about their presentations, they need to be comfortable with what they are saying and how they are saying it.

Presentation Practice Tips

- Think back with students about scientists' meetings held throughout the year to generate ideas for how they can effectively talk about their work. In many ways, scientists' meetings are ongoing rehearsals for students' KIC presentations.

- Susan Wells models an ineffective, unprofessional presentation and then analyzes the presentation with her class. This allows students to view, in a nonthreatening way, the kinds of behavior that are inappropriate for a professional presentation.

- Videotape practice sessions so that students can observe their presentations and make revisions based on their own critiques.

- Invite other classes or guests to the classroom so that students can practice in front of a live audience. This can help them make adjustments with their voices, pacing, and demonstration of materials.

- Invite students to provide written feedback to their peers on strengths and areas that need clarification or improvement.

- Students should also rehearse as audience members. Model asking good questions and develop a set of criteria for crafting a question about someone's presentation. Caution students against repeating the same question for every group. A good audience member is a thinking audience member!

Biographical Sketch

Moderators for each session at KIC will introduce each group before its presentation. In order to facilitate the introductions, each student should prepare a brief biographical sketch and bring it with him or her to his or her presentation to give to the moderator. A biographical sketch form is included in Appendix C, page 138.

Audience Skills

In addition to helping students become effective presenters, KIC provides a wonderful opportunity for students to learn how to be effective members of the audience. Audience members are expected to be active listeners and to ask thoughtful questions as part of each presentation, just as real scientists listen to and question each other in a respectful way. This too takes practice.

Maureen Hoyer brainstorms questions with her students to prepare for KIC and evaluates what types of questions are effective. Betty Lobe and Susan Wells include a practice question-and-answer period during presentation rehearsals so that students can practice being the questioners and the respondents. Teachers should do whatever works best, for their students. The ability to be an effective listener is an essential part of KIC and perhaps a forgotten component of literacy.

What happens after KIC?

As stated previously, KIC is not an end. In many ways, it is actually a beginning, and the time following KIC is as important as all the time devoted to preparing for KIC. Post-KIC is a wonderful time to unpack the experience, share memorable moments, reflect on the whole process, think about what might be done differently, and plan next steps.

In addition to revisiting KIC in discussions, many teachers ask students and parents to complete surveys to reflect on the experience. Sample parent and student survey forms are provided in Appendices N and O, pages 150 and 151. Feedback can be very helpful in planning future KICs.

It's also helpful for teachers to self-reflect on the KIC experience. What worked well? What might you do differently?

How can I keep track of what needs to be done to prepare for KIC?

Every teacher develops her own organization system, but there are a few resources to help you. A teacher checklist is provided in Appendix G (see page 142) that summarizes the key tasks involved in preparing for KIC. Chapter 10 may also be helpful in providing you with information about hosting KIC.

There is no doubt that KIC requires dedication and hard work by teachers and students. So why should I do one?

The following are just a few of the many and varied benefits teachers have observed through the years. Participating in KIC helps students

- increase critical-thinking skills
- apply thinking skills across content areas
- increase effective communication skills
- ask better and more varied questions
- demand more evidence to support the claims of others—including authors and scientists
- become better writers
- increase their interest in science (especially girls and reluctant learners)
- boost their self-confidence—KIC can be a tremendous equalizer, providing an opportunity for students who have difficulty in other areas to shine
- improve their social skills
- become successful learners

References

Martin, Jacqueline Briggs. 1998. *Snowflake Bentley*. Boston: Houghton Mifflin.

6 *Connecting Science and Literacy Through Inquiry and KIC*

Science and literacy are not mutually exclusive entities, even though we may communicate that idea because of the nature of compartmentalized instruction. Whenever possible, it is helpful to model and provide practice for students in integrated instruction that demonstrates how one area of study connects to and supports another. Real scientists incorporate extensive literacy skills throughout each step of the scientific process, including research, documentation, and presentation of their investigations. It seems only natural, then, that we should engage in meaningful reading and writing as part of science and explore the world of science as part of literacy instruction. The following questions relate to science and literacy and the answers provide strategies for instruction that supports both.

How does inquiry support literacy?

Written language provides essential opportunities for students to learn how claims, evidence, and warrants work in science. It is through reading and writing that students are given time to think systematically and carefully about their assumptions and those of other scientists. Students need to read a variety of informational texts to gather background knowledge that will support their research. Students need to write to document and make sense of their data. Students need to communicate to share their findings. Inquiry supports literacy in the most authentic way—students have a real purpose, a genuine need for developing and using literacy skills.

I generally choose fiction for read-alouds. How can read-alouds support science as well as literacy?

Science-related literature, especially nonfiction, is often an untapped resource for read-aloud book selections. By choosing well-written, engaging science books, teachers provide the opportunity to introduce students to new genres of literature at the same time that they model reading and thinking strategies that foster critical thinking. Science-related books motivate students. Emergent and avid readers alike often select nature and science books as their favorite genre of literature. Read-alouds of these texts provide students with the opportunity to experience informational literature that may be beyond their independent reading level, an opportunity that teachers already frequently provide for fictional literature. Read-alouds can be used to

- introduce lessons
- provide an introduction to new concepts and increase science vocabulary
- supplement the abstract nature of science textbooks' explanations
- invite conversation and generate questions for discussion and investigations
- model scientific thinking
- provide content to support hands-on investigations
- model different problem-solving approaches to science that may support students in their own scientific investigations
- help students examine colorful illustrations and photographs, which can tell a story beyond the words on the page

When the teacher reads aloud from a science trade book, the read-aloud process tends to become an interactive rather than a passive experience for the students. As the read-aloud progresses, students and teacher alike make discoveries and connections and even develop new questions that need to be shared, resulting in a read-aloud/think-aloud format. Through this interactive format, students learn that reading nonfiction is not a passive information dump, but is instead fertile ground for discussion and sharing. As a teacher reads, he pauses to reflect aloud on his wonderings, which in turn both models and inspires wonderings in his students.

Preparing for a Read-Aloud

Every read-aloud experience is unique, but there are some basic preparatory guidelines to think about:

- Choose a book or section of a book that lends itself to being read aloud. Does the text flow? Is the topic engaging? Are there opportunities for stopping points to wonder aloud? Does the text inspire questions?

- Gather background information on the author. Many authors of science-related literature have interesting backgrounds that *may* inspire students in their own scientific or literary endeavors. Many now have their own websites.

- Locate relevant artifacts, illustrations, or other hands-on materials that might support the text.

- Think about the focus for your read-aloud and mark "talking points" (places in the text where you want to stop and reflect or ask questions) to support that focus. This focus could be science related or related to author's craft or literary features, depending upon your purpose. The focus shouldn't be limited to just *recall of content*. The focus should be on *how*—how the reader makes meaning from text; how the author uses the craft of writing and text features to convey meaning to the reader, and so on.

- Develop open-ended questions to stimulate students' minds and imaginations. By engaging in interactive dialogue during the read-aloud, students are active participants in the text, rather than passive listeners.

- Identify any key words, concepts, or vocabulary to discuss in context as you read the text.

- Plan any related activities to follow or precede the read-aloud.

- Think about connections to other literature (intertextual connections)—between authors, topics, or genres. Collect related books for a classroom reading display.

- Practice reading your selection aloud, handling the book for your audience and using your stops.

For suggestions for read-alouds about scientists and their work and scientific processes, see Chapter 11. For more information on science-related read-alouds and think-alouds, visit the ESIP website at *esiponline.org/classroom/foundations/reading/readalouds.html*.

How can I incorporate science into literature circles?

Literature circles tend to look and work a bit differently from classroom to classroom. In spite of the variations that you might find, there are some similarities and core elements in literature circles. Literature circles are, in fact, the classroom kid-friendly versions of adult book clubs and discussion groups. Although traditional book clubs focus on fiction or narrative text, here we offer some recommendations for your science trade book literature circle. Literature circles are near-perfect vehicles for sparking group inquiry projects, because inquiry is based on asking questions, sharing ideas, and exploring possibilities.

- Rather than focus on fiction, turn to nonfiction, in particular science nonfiction, for book choices.
- Put together a text set for your current science unit of study. Have students select from this list of books so that while they are reading and discussing the book, they also are reading and discussing relevant science content.
- If the focus is on a particular type of book, select science-related books that fit your language arts focus. Studying biography? Use books about scientists and their work. Focusing on poetry? Select science-related poetry collections.
- Use literature circles to discuss and compare the various ways that science information on the same topic is presented booking different books.
- Have students examine the various choices that authors make by having each group read a different book about the same science notable. Afterward, have the groups share and compare what they learned about the person from the books they read.

More information on science literature circles can be found at *esiponline.org/classroom/foundations/reading/science_lit_circle.html*.

What strategies are helpful to teach students about selecting informational books for independent reading and research?

At every Kids' Inquiry Conference, students explain why they pursued a particular question or investigation. Although their reasons vary, a large number of the young scientists begin their explanations with "I read this book . . ." Independent reading can be the spark that starts the inquiry engine, but first students need to be presented with quality informational literature and the strategies that work for reading and understanding it.

Browsing Strategies

Too often, a lot of time is spent modeling and instructing students in the reading process, and the process of selecting a book is overlooked or only lightly touched on. Selecting a just-right book can be especially important as children begin browsing informational texts. The reading level and the content can be challenging and the reader must be motivated and interested enough to persevere. The teacher should model successful strategies for choosing a just-right text.

- Think about your own selection process. Bring in a few books that you have selected to read as well as a few that you opted not to read.
- Talk about and model what you did when you were book browsing.
- Share your reasons for choosing one book but putting aside another.
- When you picked up a book, what attracted you to it? Cover? Length? Author? Title?
- When you opened it, what did you do? Did you fan through the pages to see if anything caught your eye? Did you look for a table of contents or an index? Did you try to read a page or two to see if you were comfortable with the text?
- Did you have a particular purpose in mind when you were looking for books? Were you looking for specific information? Looking for a book to read for pleasure? Looking for books by a familiar author?
- Direct students to focus on a book's visuals. Do they like the illustrations? Do they find the photographs fascinating? Do the tables provide the information they are seeking?
- Allow students time to browse. Encourage them to look more closely at books that capture their interest. Have them read a few pages to self-assess readability.
- Show students how to compare texts by looking at the information in different books on the same topic. Is the information the same? Are the formats and styles different or the same? Which books would they prefer to read?

Book Talks

Once the students have begun selecting their own books during book browsing, encourage them to share their finds with the rest of the class through book talks. Book talks are opportunities for students to share the books they love with the class. They prepare a persuasive "commercial" for the book by noting interesting information, helpful text features, fascinating illustrations, and other aspects of the book they found particularly enjoyable and/or informative. The book talk serves several purposes:

- It encourages students to read a variety of texts.
- It provides an opportunity for students to orally present to a large audience of peers.

- It creates an authentic purpose for students to prepare a brief summary and persuasive paragraph.
- Additionally, the book talk allows the teacher to monitor student progress in independent reading, communication skills, and interests.

Where can I find quality science-related trade books for my classroom?

See Chapter 11 for more about science trade books—suggested titles, how to find them, and how to evaluate them.

What exactly are scientist's notebooks?

Writing becomes a valuable element of the inquiry classroom as exploration moves into investigation. Students need a place to record their observations and questions, reflect on their experiences, and track data from their investigations and from other information sources. By keeping a written record, they have a way to look back, revise, and plan for next steps. Jeanne Reardon has developed the scientist's notebook as a way of helping young scientists keep track of their two most important activities: (1) documenting research and investigations and (2) asking questions.

The scientist's notebook is a record of inquiry; it is a source of information to be used in discussions and as a reference for writing expanded explanations, informative articles, and reports for the community of classroom scientists. The notebook is a guide to read and reread; it's a way to collect and organize

- questions raised; questions answered
- procedures followed; materials used
- data collected
- references consulted
- explanations and theories generated
- personal reflections and wonderings
- scientific drawings, tables, and charts

This ongoing record becomes part of a narrative—the student's story of his inquiry with the student himself as the primary audience of these pages of lists, ideas, numbers, symbols, and drawings.

For more information on scientists' notebooks, visit *esiponline.org/classroom/foundations/writing/notebook.html*.

How can I incorporate inquiry with writing workshop?

Throughout the inquiry process, there are many, many opportunities for authentic writing. From the very start students are recording questions, observations, data, and background information as part of the explorations and investigations. Minilesson opportunities range from teaching strategies for organizing and recording data to how to take background notes from text. As students fill their science notebooks or journals, the notebooks become valuable primary sources of real information that can be used to teach students how to craft informational writing pieces.

To support informational writing, spend some time with well-known authors of nonfiction children's trade books in order to study how investigations and research are presented in a narrative form. Text features such as photographs, illustrations, diagrams, charts, and graphs play large roles in these books; how can your young scientists incorporate these into their writing? Select a well-known author (visit *esiponline.org/books/authors/authors.html* for information about authors) and visit the library to borrow a collection of his or her titles for your class. Ask students to work together to determine the elements of the author's craft that make these books more interesting than a textbook, for instance. Then encourage your students to use these texts as models for their own narrative writing about their investigations. This activity becomes a powerful support for the *KIC Journal* articles students will write later in the year.

How do *KIC Journals* support science and literacy goals?

KIC Journals were born out of a fervent desire on the part of KIC participants to be able to read about the presentations they were unable to attend. Much as scientists publish their work in journals, KIC participants publish their work so that others may read about it. Over the years, *KIC Journals* have come to be so much more than just a record of missed presentations. *KIC Journals* are sources of pride for their authors and sources of inspiration for the scientists that follow, and they are terrific tools for introducing inquiry in the classroom.

Here are a few of the ways *KIC Journals* are used in the classroom:

- Early in the school year, *KIC Journals* from previous years are introduced as catalysts for inquiry and questions. As Charles Pearce states, "I bring in *KIC Journals* to look at questions kids have asked over the years . . . That's the first introduction . . . examine questions that other kids ask."

- Teachers use *KIC Journals* as authentic primary source texts for reading. In addition to becoming aware of the investigation process, challenges, and successes and failures, students reading the *KIC Journal*s will begin critical analyses of the information presented. Are the procedures detailed enough to duplicate? Does the data support the student's conclusions? Are the observations presented in a clear and logical manner?

- *KIC Journal*s are used as resources for student research as kids conduct their own investigations. Students may compare data results, adapt a graphic organizer for their own purpose, or check the references for a book or website that might be helpful to their own investigations.

- Often *KIC Journal*s are used to introduce the conference to students. Students can read and discuss what they notice. How did participants go about their investigations? Where did their questions come from? What problems did they encounter along the way?

- Since no two articles look exactly alike, journal articles provide examples of informational writing and invite discussion about the craft of informational writing. How is the information organized? What words are particularly effective in communicating information? How did the author weave data in with text? What makes a particular article compelling or inviting? What hooks work well to entice the reader?

For more on guidelines for writing journal articles, see Appendix J, page 146. Sample *KIC Journal* articles are also available at the KIC website *(esiponline.learnserver.net/kic).*

7 Assessment in the Inquiry Classroom

Opportunities for assessment are abundant and important to the inquiry process. Students generate questions, make plans, produce written documents, and share ideas in a forum that invites and, frankly, requires reflection and revision. Throughout the process, teachers are observing and challenging students and students are doing the same with each other. This chapter addresses questions related to assessment.

How is assessment integrated into the inquiry process?

As previously discussed, a critical part of inquiry is making public findings and supporting those findings with evidence. In both scientists' meetings and debriefing sessions, students are invited to share their work with the community of scientists (classmates). Fellow scientists challenge claims and raise questions, holding students accountable for their findings. Students are asked to revisit their thinking and look ever so closely at their work. This level of peer interaction fosters self-assessment. Students wonder, What do I know? What evidence do I have to support that? How carefully have I documented my findings? Assessment, in this context, is an integral part of inquiry.

How can I assess how my students are doing as they work on their inquiry investigations?

The following are a few assessment strategies that many teachers find helpful in documenting student progress and planning instruction to support students' needs.

Checklists and Rating Scales
Checklists provide a written description of observable behaviors or criteria that can be assessed throughout the year. Documentation can vary. A few ideas include using a check-box format to indicate the attainment of a

specific skill; using frequency descriptors (often, sometimes, seldom, never) to periodically review all the behaviors; and recording supporting notes with dates next to indicators as evidence of attainment. (See Figure 7–1.)

Anecdotal Records

A record of observations of student behaviors over time is a helpful tool in looking for patterns of student behavior. Anecdotal records can be collected in a variety of ways:

- composition book for daily entries
- mall reporter's notepads for individual students
- Sticky notes inside a file folder on a clipboard, prelabeled for each student
- self-adhesive address labels for recording short notes that can be pasted into a binder under each child's section later in the day
- index cards that can be carried in a small box and refiled
- note-taking packets distributed to students that have a section for teacher comments at the end

Interviews and Student Conferences

Interviews and conferences provide teachers and students an opportunity to dialogue about specific skills and behaviors of scientific inquiry. Students prepare for conferences by gathering evidence to support the focus of the conference. During the conference, the teacher and student can discuss the topic, ask questions, and set goals. (See Figure 7–2.)

Evaluation of Students' Written Work

Students' written work is an important source of data. Jeanne Reardon's students record their observations, questions, and reflections in their scientists' notebooks. Charles Pearce's students write in discovery logs and dialogue journals to record their data, questions, and thoughts during their inquiry periods. These resources, as well as pieces from writing workshop, more formal reports, responses to writing prompts, and various other writings, are a rich source of data for assessing students' scientific thinking and understanding of inquiry. Examples of student-authored work include

- discovery logs
- summaries of progress
- self-assessments
- scientist's notebooks
- *KIC Journal* articles

Inquiry Science Indicators Checklist

For _____

This student:	Often	Sometimes	Seldom	Never
1. Asks testable questions	_____	_____	_____	_____
2. Designs fair tests to answer questions	_____	_____	_____	_____
3. Gathers data in an organized and logical manner	_____	_____	_____	_____
4. Identifies and seeks additional materials	_____	_____	_____	_____
5. Reads for additional information related to an investigation	_____	_____	_____	_____
6. Exhibits an understanding of variables in an experiment	_____	_____	_____	_____
7. Exhibits understanding and use of a control	_____	_____	_____	_____
8. Translates observations into usable data	_____	_____	_____	_____
9. Discusses ongoing investigations with others	_____	_____	_____	_____
10. Exhibits perseverance, especially on investigations with unexpected results	_____	_____	_____	_____
11. Compares data with others doing similar investigations	_____	_____	_____	_____
12. Records data for future use	_____	_____	_____	_____
13. Asks new questions based upon new data	_____	_____	_____	_____
14. Creates or modifies models	_____	_____	_____	_____
15. Engages in self-directed investigations	_____	_____	_____	_____
16. Makes entries in the Book of Discoveries	_____	_____	_____	_____
17. Makes connections between different investigations	_____	_____	_____	_____
18. Expresses interest in replicating the investigations of others	_____	_____	_____	_____

Figure 7–1. Assessment checklist

How do I decide if a KIC proposal, presentation, or journal article is of sufficient quality for KIC?

Each classroom teacher is her own mini KIC Committee. It is the classroom teacher who reviews the proposals for the conference, edits the articles for the *KIC Journal*, and helps assess the quality of her students'

Science Conference

Name: _____ Date:_____

Questions:

- Prompted by observations, curiosity, confusions, unanticipated findings, explanations, tests, data
- About own work, work of others, reading
- During minilessons, explorations/investigations, scientists' meetings, conversations, and discussions

Scientists' Notebook:

- Includes questions, scientific drawings, data collections, observations, descriptions of procedures, lists, comments, plans, tests, reflections, response to prompts
- Used to ask new questions, record data, describe procedures, build explanations, plan next steps of investigations, make connections, report work in progress

Explanations:

- Based on evidence from investigations, resources
- Compared to current thinking of science
- Revised in response to new evidence
- Considers others possible explanations
- Written, presented to class, respond to questions and comments

Explorations and Investigations:

- Records work in scientists' notebook
- Uses tools and/or scientific instruments
- Knows and uses several ways of recording and analyzing data
- Builds on the work of others
- Describes investigations in a way that others can replicate

Resources:

- Uses books, magazines, news articles, people, materials, WWW
- Used for wide reading, background information, models, to confirm or discredit findings and explanations
- Evaluation based on publication date, credibility of author

Scientists' Meetings:

- Reports work in progress, findings, explanations
- Considers classmates' response to own work
- Listens and responds to other students' work

Plans:

Figure 7–2. Science conference topics

presentations as the day of the conference approaches. An understanding of the conference goals (as described on pages 11–12) is essential. In addition, each teacher must decide on her own set of expectations for the conference based upon the abilities of her students. As I review the proposals that are submitted to the KIC Committee, I asked three critical questions.

First, will the proposed investigation place the student in any danger? Materials or procedures that are unsafe must be discouraged. It is essential that the students understand the topic of investigation well enough to know where to draw limits concerning safe practices. It is the classroom teacher's responsibility to monitor the ongoing steps of each investigation.

Second, will animals be used in the investigation and, if so, will their safety and comfort be guaranteed throughout the project? It is our moral obligation to treat *all* animals in humane ways, and we must communicate these beliefs to our students. Guidelines can be found in the NSTA position statement for working with animals in the classroom (1991).

Finally, will the investigation yield student-gathered data that can be analyzed and replicated? A proposal in which the student describes an authentic question with detailed ways to answer it through an investigation or observation is one that would, in most cases, be accepted for the conference. Even if the question seems simplistic or shallow, if actual data are generated, a story of scientific inquiry will emerge. On the other hand, research-type questions, those that can be answered only by reviewing the data of someone else, are to be discouraged. KIC presentations are not book reports.

Responses to the proposals are based upon these questions. If a problem is apparent, a letter from the KIC Committee will express the concern and invite the student to resubmit with revisions.

As the presentations are being planned, the classroom teacher coaches each student to adequately tell the story of inquiry. It is our goal to make sure each student is prepared and will not be embarrassed by lack of detail or faulty data. As a guide, I share with my students five parts of an inquiry presentation:

1. the original question and how it was inspired
2. background information on the topic (what others have discovered)
3. a description of the investigation with sufficient details for replication
4. the data
5. additional questions for others to pursue

It helps to practice the presentations in class or for other students in the school. Feedback can be provided to the presenters with a form like that shown in Appendix Q (see page 153). Students are able to fine-tune their presentations based upon the responses of others.

The article for the *KIC Journal* also tells the story of inquiry and discovery. Its assessment by the classroom teacher can be based upon the expectations for other formal classroom writing assignments. A student guide for writing the KIC article can be found in Appendix J (see page 146).

As they evaluate the proposals, presentations, and articles, it is important for teachers to trust their own judgment. If a proposal seems right, it probably is. Empowering students to tell their stories at the conference also means empowering the teachers who are planning that conference. You know your students better than anyone. Who better to make the important decisions about KIC than you!

References

National Science Teachers Association (NSTA). 1991. "Guidelines for Responsible Use of Animals in the Classroom." Retrieved from *www.nsta.org/positionstatement&psid=2.*

8 *Supporting Science and Literacy Standards Through KIC*

No discussion about KIC would be complete without looking at how the Kids' Inquiry Conference and inquiry support national science and literacy standards. The following questions address the National Science Education Standards and the IRA/NCTE Content Standards for the English Language Arts, respectively, and provide examples of how those standards are supported by an inquiry conference.

How do the National Science Education Standards support an inquiry conference for kids?

The National Science Standards are clear about inquiry. Science instruction must include an inquiry component. "Inquiry into authentic questions generated from student experiences is the central strategy for teaching science." (NRC 1996, 31)

In April 2000, the National Research Council released *Inquiry and the National Science Education Standards* as an addendum to the original standards. This volume, focusing on the importance of inquiry in the classroom, provided additional details about two parts of the content standards for science as inquiry: (1) fundamental abilities necessary to do scientific inquiry and (2) fundamental understandings about scientific inquiry. Classroom experiences, which lead to the Kids' Inquiry Conference, parallel the activities and scientific thinking stressed in the standards. Following are the content standards and descriptions of two similar student investigations that show how participating in KIC supports these standards.

Content Standard for Science as Inquiry: Fundamental Abilities Necessary to Do Scientific Inquiry

Grades K–4

- *Ask a question about objects, organisms, and events in the environment.* Peter had a question about seeds that his teacher helped him write on the classroom question board. His question was How long does it take for a seed to grow? His teacher helped him refine his question to How long does it take for a radish seed to grow?

- *Plan and conduct a simple investigation.* Peter planted several radish seeds and planned to observe their growth.

- *Employ simple equipment and tools to gather data and extend the senses.* In his journal, Peter recorded the day the seeds were planted and noted when they began to grow. He then measured the seedlings daily and recorded their progress until flowers appeared. Peter then wondered about fertilizer and how it might enhance growth. He decided to plant more seeds in separate containers and fertilize those in one container and observe differences in growth.

- *Use data to construct a reasonable explanation.* From his observed data, Peter explained that fertilizer did not seem to speed up germination but did seem to make the seedlings grow at a faster rate.

- *Communicate investigations and explanations.* Peter reported his data about seed growth and the effects of fertilizer at the Kids' Inquiry Conference.

Grades 5–8

- *Identify questions that can be answered through scientific investigations.* Sarah was curious about the effects of salt water on the growth of plants. On the question board, she wrote, "How will salt water affect the growth of grass?" Her question was identified as a testable question that could be answered through an investigation.

- *Design and conduct a scientific investigation.* Sarah and two friends designed an investigation in which they would compare ten different strengths of salt water as they used the salt water to water samples of grass.

- *Use appropriate tools and techniques to gather, analyze, and interpret data.* The team decided upon the intensity of salt water and prepared ten containers of varying strengths. They gathered ten samples of identical grass and watered each sample daily with the same amounts of the respective salt water. They recorded daily analysis based upon observations of each grass sample.

- *Develop descriptions, explanations, predictions, and models using evidence.* Initially the team thought that the grass watered with fresh water (no salt) would remain the most healthy (greener with vigorous growth) while the grass watered with the highest concentration of salt would not survive. The observations were somewhat different. Although the grass watered with the highest concentration of salt withered and died, the grass watered with water containing a trace of salt seemed to fare better than the grass watered with fresh water (no salt).

- *Think critically and logically to make the relationships between evidence and explanations.* The team decided that for some reason, a small amount of salt enhanced the growth of the grass.

- *Recognize and analyze alternative explanations and predictions.* The team realized that their original predictions were not supported by the data and planned to try the investigation with other plants.

- *Communicate scientific procedures and explanations.* The story told at the Kids' Inquiry Conference and published in the *KIC Journal* explained the original question, methods of investigation, and the observed data. The team offered the seemingly puzzling results of the investigation to others to replicate and try to explain.

Consider the student investigations just described and how they relate to the fundamental understandings about scientific inquiry.

Content Standard for Science as Inquiry: Fundamental Understandings About Scientific Inquiry

Grades K–4

- *Scientific investigations involve asking and answering a question and comparing the answer with what scientists already know about the world.* The link with nonfiction trade books is an important one. As students read about the discoveries of others, they compare what is already known with the results of their own investigations.

- *Scientists use different kinds of investigations depending on the questions they are trying to answer.* As students share their questions and investigations with one another, they come to realize that a fair test may require differing means of investigating. Simple instruments such as magnifiers, thermometers, and rulers provide more information than scientists obtain using only their senses. Traditional classroom instruction is not to be replaced by exclusive use of inquiry methods. Indeed, students must be taught the use of scientific tools so that their own meaningful inquiry can follow.

- *Scientists develop explanations using observations (evidence) and what they already know about the world (scientific knowledge).* Prior knowledge is crucial, not only for the development of questions but also for relevant explanations of data. That knowledge can come from the established science curriculum, science trade books, or from teacher explanations.

- *Scientists make the results of their investigations public; they describe the investigations in ways that enable others to repeat the investigations.* Students report the results of their investigations at KIC and record their stories in the *KIC Journal*. Readers of the KIC articles critically analyze the descriptions of methods and decide if sufficient information is provided to replicate the investigations. This assessment of others leads to a more thorough self-assessment as students write new articles.

- *Scientists review and ask questions about the results of other scientists' work.* An important part of KIC is the question-and-discussion time that follows each presentation. Students are invited to participate in discussions of described investigations.

Grades 5–8

- *Different kinds of questions suggest different kinds of scientific investigations.*

- *Current scientific knowledge and understanding guide scientific investigations.* The science curriculum is important as an inspiration for testable questions that may lead to investigations and discoveries.

- *Mathematics is important in all aspects of scientific inquiry.* As students record their observations, they come to realize the importance of numerical data. Presenting those data quantitatively enhances credibility. As students analyze what is convincing to themselves, they see the importance of mathematics in the gathering and display of their own data.

- *Technology used to gather data enhances accuracy and allows scientists to analyze and quantify results of investigations.*

- *Scientific explanations emphasize evidence, have logically consistent arguments, and use scientific principles, models, and theories.* Students strive for credibility. They are the experts because the investigations are their own and their explanations must be logically portrayed.

- *Science advances through legitimate skepticism.* Students are encouraged to question one another. They are astutely aware of what is fair and are able to distinguish a fair test from one that is biased. Being skeptical means needing to be convinced. As students come to understand how they are convinced themselves, they come to understand how to convince others.

- *Scientific investigations sometimes result in new ideas and phenomena for study, generate new methods or procedures for an investigation, or develop new technologies to improve the collection of data.* The use of the *KIC Journal*s containing articles from past years has inspired students to embark on investigations based upon the gathered data of others. As a result, new questions have been asked with innovative means of data collection. Our scientific community has not only been developed within one class during one particular year but has been extended from year to year, with students building on the investigations and discoveries of those who preceded them.

Students in classrooms in which inquiry is valued as described in the standards are, by default, prepared for an inquiry conference. Conversely, students who are being prepared for an inquiry conference are naturally meeting the goals set out in the standards.

How do the content standards for English Language Arts support an inquiry conference for kids?

Teachers whose classes have participated in KIC have often remarked on the amount of language arts instruction that occurs throughout the inquiry process. In fact, many teachers schedule their inquiry investigation or exploration periods during the language arts block for that very reason. We have provided a sampling of the language arts standards developed by the International Reading Association and the National Council of Teachers of English so that you can assess for yourself the alignment possibilities between language arts and KIC.

The International Reading Association and the National Council of Teachers of English have developed content standards with three specific goals:

- to develop verbal ability
- to guarantee creative and effective English curricula
- to define core elements in the teaching and learning of language

These three goals are designed to ensure that all students receive a variety of experiences and instruction designed to prepare them to be fully literate and effective communicators.

The complete set of IRA/NCTE Content Standards for the English Language Arts can be found online at *www.readwritethink.org*, a joint project of IRA, NCTE, and MarcoPolo. We have listed several of them here to demonstrate the link between inquiry in the classroom and national goals for language arts instruction.

Standard One

Students read a wide range of print and nonprint texts to build an understanding of texts, of themselves, and of the cultures of the United

States and the world; to acquire new information; to respond to the needs and demands of society and the workplace, and for personal fulfillment. Among these texts are fiction and nonfiction, classic and contemporary works.

- Students involved in the exploration and investigation of a question they are interested in will seek to acquire new information by
  - reading science trade books
  - reading newspapers
  - using technology
  - accessing other sources of reference material and resources
- Students tend to select topics directly relating to the needs and demands of their own lives.
- As a result of this exposure to a variety of materials, students are more likely to experience and select informational literature for personal enjoyment.

Standard Three

Students apply a wide range of strategies to comprehend, interpret, evaluate, and appreciate texts. They draw on their prior experience, their interactions with other readers and writers, their knowledge of word meaning and of other texts, their word identification strategies, and their understanding of textual features (e.g., sound-letter correspondence, sentence structure, context, graphics).

- Because students have a need to acquire and apply information in order to further their investigations, they have a genuine motivation to develop strategies for understanding a variety of text, both print and nonprint. Some skills and strategies that are actively applied include, but are not limited to
  - vocabulary skills
  - comprehension strategies for both narrative and informational print texts, as well as visual, technological, and audio media
  - strategies for analyzing text features—graphs, images, diagrams, and so on—and applying them in their own writing
- Students develop critical evaluation skills as they determine which materials are useful for informing and furthering investigations and which materials are not.
- Finally, students also apply these strategies in dialogues with classmates, educators, and other persons (scientists and other experts) who assist with research and materials for investigations.

Standard Four

Students adjust their use of spoken, written, and visual language (e.g., conventions, style, vocabulary) to communicate effectively with a variety of audiences and for different purposes.

- This standard includes the elements of spoken and visual language that are often undervalued in traditional English language arts instruction, but are strongly represented in an inquiry-based classroom. Communication is central to the inquiry conference. Students actively document their explorations and investigations in scientist's notebooks and discovery logs and discuss that work with their peers in scientists meetings. In preparation for KIC, communication skills continue to develop as students
  - document the process and data they collect throughout their investigations
  - create an advertising blurb to entice audience members to sign up for their presentations
  - prepare *KIC Journal* articles, published accounts of their questions and findings
  - present at KIC, which requires not only oral communication but also demonstration materials and audio/visual media communication as well

Inquiry in the classroom is truly an authentic and inclusive method of instruction that can be applied to all elements of this standard.

Standard Five

Students employ a wide range of strategies as they write and use different writing process elements appropriately to communicate with different audiences for a variety of purposes.

If we use Megan Dieckman's story as an example for this standard, it is apparent that a KIC investigation can lead students to use a variety of strategies and elements to communicate effectively. Megan had to

- complete an application
- record data
- communicate electronically with peers at other schools regarding their investigations
- write a letter communicating with a business to request information and supplies
- write a blurb advertising her group's KIC presentation

- write a journal article for the KIC presentation
- design a variety of methods to present data to an audience composed of students, parents, educators, university personnel, and professional scientists

Finally, Megan applied this standard and her previous experience with KIC to write a chapter for this book, documenting the value of inquiry from a student's point of view.

Standard Seven

Students conduct research on issues and interests by generating ideas and questions, and by posing problems. They gather, evaluate, and synthesize data from a variety of sources (e.g., print and nonprint texts, artifacts, people) to communicate their discoveries in ways that suit their purposes and audience.

- The first step in any investigation is gathering information, applying it, and gathering more information. This standard is clearly observed at work throughout the year as students are learning what sparks a question, where to find information, and how to plan and carry out an investigation.
- Students must be able locate data using a variety of resources, evaluate the quality of data, apply their findings to their original question, and finally communicate this process to group members, classmates, and an audience of young scientists like themselves.

Standard Twelve

Students use spoken, written, and visual language to accomplish their own purposes (e.g., for learning, enjoyment, persuasion, and the exchange of information).

This is the essence of KIC. Students have spent months in pursuit of their own questions and investigations. This is their opportunity to present their accomplishments, and they relish the chance. Students will arrive with artifacts to share, personally prepared charts and other visual aids, even videotaped footage of their investigations. Why? Because they were invested in an experience that they truly owned and they want to share it with others.

References

International Reading Association (IRA) and National Council of Teachers of English (NCTE). 1996. "IRA/NCTE Standards for the

English Language Arts." Retrieved from *www.readwritethink.org/standards/ index.html.*

National Research Council (NRC). 1996. *The National Science Education Standards.* Washington, DC: National Academy Press.

———. 2000. *Inquiry and the National Science Education Standards.* Washington, DC: National Academy Press.

9 *Learning to Think Outside the Box: A Student's KIC Story*

Megan Dieckman

Megan Dieckman was a student participant in the 1995 Kids' Inquiry Conference when she was in fourth grade. She was a student in Maureen Hoyer's class at Woodbridge Elementary School in Baltimore, Maryland. The following is Meg's story of KIC from a student's perspective. She shares the origins of her questions, discusses her partnership with three fellow students (Stewart Wolfe, Chase Gilbert, and Joe Conroy), and talks about the KIC experience, then and now.

This story may be photocopied for classroom use to share with students.

When I was growing up, I was very shy. I enjoyed school, especially science, but I didn't volunteer to participate in activities. That all changed in fourth grade thanks to an inspirational teacher, Mrs. Hoyer, and a creative science project called the Kids' Inquiry Conference. My shyness and my enthusiasm for science collided and the result continues to influence my life today. (See Figure 9–1.)

Mrs. Hoyer also loved science, and she communicated that love by challenging us to explore the world around us. She inspired us to ask questions and think creatively about problem solving. From the first day of school, inquiry and reading science trade books were integral parts of our classroom. Within each unit we learned in science, Mrs. Hoyer wove a hands-on aspect for us to explore. For example, in our rocks and minerals unit, we not only learned about them but read books and even got to see the inside of geodes. Also, early in the school year, she invited Mr. Carico, a scientist, to our classroom. One of the many experiments he demonstrated introduced us to a substance called a polymer. "What is it?" I thought. Little did I know three boys in my class were thinking the same thing.

Just before winter break, Mrs. Hoyer told our class about a very special project called the Kids' Inquiry Conference (KIC, for short). This student-directed science conference invited budding young scientists to conduct their own investigations during the school year and present their findings later in the year at the University of Maryland, Baltimore County. My initial reaction bordered on hysteria. While excited at the prospect of

Figure 9–1.   Megan, age 10, working on polymer experiment

conducting my own science investigation, the thought of making a presentation in front of a large group of people absolutely terrified me.

Mrs. Hoyer gave our class the task of brainstorming ideas for KIC over winter break. I thought about doing investigations on rocks, bubbles, or crystals, but I already knew a great deal about them. Knowing that I would be spending a significant portion of the rest of my year learning more about this topic, I thought very hard about what to choose. After much contemplation, I came to the conclusion that I wanted to research something I knew nothing about—a real challenge. I remembered Mr. Carico's visit and my curiosity about polymers. The more I thought about it, the more I knew I had found my investigation. Now I needed to find my courage.

After arriving back from winter break, our class discussed the ideas we had come up with. Other class members suggested bubbles, batteries, magnets, balloons, water, water clocks, and our favorite: mold. I suggested polymers, and, to my astonishment, three boys excitedly responded they wanted to investigate polymers as well. A group project was born. Yikes! I went from being scared to sit next to them and terrified at the thought of speaking to them to being partners with three of them, all in a matter of a few fateful minutes.

I think Mrs. Hoyer sensed my initial uneasiness, especially since our group was the only co-ed group in the class. She supplied us with constant encouragement and a good dose of humor, reminding us that we should think of ourselves as a groundbreaking force to be reckoned with. Whatever she did, it worked. Stewart, Joey, Chase, and I started to act as a team and the research began. (See Figure 9–2.)

Our first task involved understanding what a polymer was, so we contacted Mr. Carico and asked him for the name of the company his polymer came from. We wrote to the company, asking for information and any samples it could provide us to use in our experiments. As we awaited a reply, we read books about polymers and designed experiments. The more research we gathered, the more information we learned, and the more experiments we did, the more questions we had. Because this was a substance we knew nothing about, everything we learned was a surprise. A critical part of this process involved our ability to document our findings so that we could share our work at the conference, and I discovered a knack for organizing data. (See Figure 9–3.)

All the other groups were immersed in their research as well. Sometimes what one group learned would benefit another group. The soap group informed us that when a particular type of soap was added to water in high concentration, it formed the consistency of a polymer. "Was it one?" we asked ourselves. This led us to look more closely at the composition of a polymer. The definition we found in a book explained that a polymer is a long strand of molecules arranged in a certain way. What? We were in the fourth grade, and we didn't have a clue what that meant.

Then my mom went to a science meeting and she brought back a book titled *Polymers Around Us*, which provided us with a lot of answers to our questions, in words we could understand. We learned that polymers surround us in our everyday lives. Common polymers include contact lenses, disposable diapers, and plastic products. At about the same time, the polymer company wrote us back and sent us not only information about the polymer Mr. Carico used but also enough samples to sustain our research for the rest of the investigation. Now we could start experimenting with this intriguing substance in earnest!

Through our background reading and our own research, we concluded that a polymer is an absorbent material, and that when it comes

Figure 9–2.   Joey, Stewart, and Chase, age 10, investigating

in contact with a liquid, it expands and absorbs the liquid. We wanted to try to apply this concept to practical uses so we designed experiments to test our understanding. We were all interested in the environment and practical applications of polymers, so we simulated a volcano eruption using baking soda and vinegar and added polymer to see the effects. We learned a great deal through trial and error. Our first explosion went everywhere (too much vinegar was the culprit), compelling Mrs. Hoyer to move our "laboratory" to the outdoor classroom. Further investigation yielded more fruitful and less messy results. We learned that if a polymer agent was added to the vinegar, the vinegar would gel, preventing the volcanic reaction from occurring. However, if the polymer was added just as the baking soda and vinegar were starting to react, the reaction would be significantly slowed down.

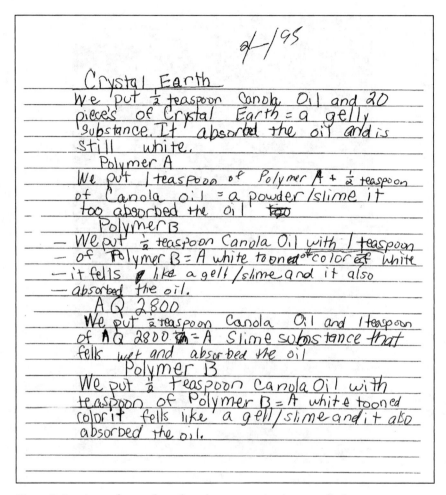

Figure 9–3.   A sample page from the polymer group's science notebook

Around February, amid our investigations, we started crafting what we were going to write in our KIC application (see Figure 9–4). After several drafts we sent the final copy to the KIC review board. We eagerly waited to hear back from them! Meanwhile we investigated the use of polymers to help with oil spill cleanups. We filled pans with water, used three different kinds of cooking oil, and used different types of polymers. The experiment failed because the polymers absorbed the water as well as the oils. We tried not to get discouraged because Mrs. Hoyer had taught us the importance of failure in scientific research. Through stories about real scientists, we learned that failure benefits scientists' understanding just as much as successes do.

In March we received our acceptance letters in the mail. We were torn between excitement and nervousness. We had been working steadily on our research since January, but we knew the time would come soon that we would have to solidify our questions and findings a bit further and start to think about what we wanted to include in our presentation. We continued our research with oil spills and also conducted some small investigations to observe how polymers reacted with other chemicals and substances. We also began writing to a group of students in another school who would also be participating in KIC, sharing our discoveries and questions. It was comforting to know that when we went to the conference we would know someone else aside from the students in our class.

Figure 9–4.   Draft of KIC application to present at KIC

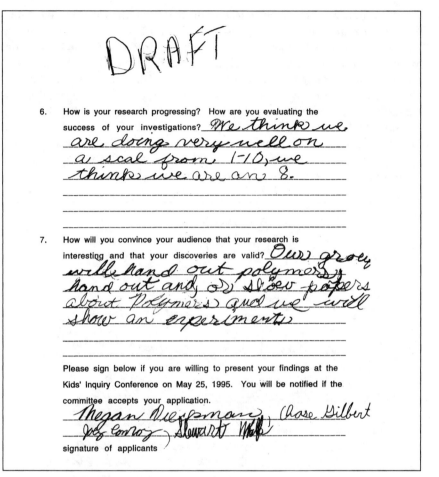

Figure 9–4.   (continued)

The time finally arrived to start planning for the conference and our presentation. We started organizing all our data and making sense of it. We wrote the advertising blurb for our presentation to entice students in other classes to sign up for our session at KIC and then we began drafting a journal article that would tell our story (see final draft in Figure 9–5). We had really compiled a lot of data and information that we needed to sift through. From this time of reflection, our presentation emerged. Then the hard work of revising, polishing, and practicing began. We had several practice sessions, and it was so important to be able to practice, especially for me, given my fear of public speaking. It was through this process that our story really became our own and we gained confidence in our ability to talk about it in a comfortable way.

Our group's dynamics wound up working perfectly. We each brought our own strengths to the team. Stewart noticed unusual things that made us continue to investigate further. Joey's hysterical humor made science ten times more fun. Chase's flexibility gave us new perspectives to consider at every turn. My organizational skills helped keep us on track and

POLYMERS

By
Megan Dieckman, Joey Conroy, Chase Gilbert, Stewart Wolfe

INTRODUCTION

Our group started on polymers because of two demonstrations. The first one was showed to us by Mr. Carico, a high school chemistry teacher. He made and showed us a polymer. Then our teacher made a polymer, and when we found out that squishy, mushy, cold stuff was a polymer, we were hooked.

DEFINITION

You're probably wondering what polymer is by now. Well, a polymer is a long chain of molecules, linked together, that repeats itself. One of the polymers we used was called A.Q. 2800. It started out dry, but when you added water it became the gel substance. The word, polymer, comes from a Greek word meaning "many parts."

EXPERIMENTS

Our main question was, what do polymers react with? We tried reacting the different polymers we had with canola oil, a vinegar and baking soda mix, sodium carbonate, calcium hydroxide, methylene blue, magnesium sulfate, citric acid, and cobalt chloride. The results of the oil spill test are on the next page.

Our vinegar and baking soda experiment didn't work out exactly as we predicted. We gathered our supplies: vinegar, baking soda, our polymer, plastic funnel, and a plastic food container. Next, we put the funnel over the container, and added two fluid ounces of vinegar, one and one fourth teaspoon of polymer, and one tablespoon of baking soda. We did this test three ways. TEST 1. We added vinegar and baking soda together, and then added polymer. The results of the test was a gelling at the bottom of the container, but the rest didn't stop. TEST 2. In this test we changed the process a little. First, we added the polymer with the baking soda. Next we added the vinegar. The results didn't change a great deal. The same thing happened except for the lack of bubbles. There was just a little less than before. TEST 3. We added polymer and vinegar together and got our gel substance. When we added baking soda nothing happened. Later after four or five minutes, the bubbling began. It started bubbling to the top of the container. Then the bubbles stayed the same height for awhile and the bubbles soon popped.

continued

Figure 9–5.   Final journal article on polymers

Another experiment we did was from a book called <u>Discovering Science Secrets</u> by Sandra Markle. Our recipe was called Yum Drops. We boiled juice with unflavored gelatin and poured it on wax paper. Then we sprinkled sugar on it. We let it cool for twenty minutes and we tried it. It may be hard to believe, but we ate a polymer. The stuff was like Jello. The chemicals and polymer tests are listed below the oil tests.

OIL TESTS

POLYMERS	OILS	RESULTS	KEY
A Q 2800	Canola	Good	
Crystal Earth	Canola	Fair	
Polymer A	Canola	Good	
Polymer B	Canola	Fair	
			Results Key:
			Great
			Good
			Fair

The oil spill tests (above) were done to see if the polymer could absorb canola oil.

CHEMICAL TESTS

Our amount of polymer changed due to the amount of the chemical we had. The dry polymer we used was called A.Q. 2,800. Here are the results.

Citric Acid 1/8 of a fl. oz. of polymer. It turned into pink glob.
Sodium Carbonate 1/4 tbsp. of polymer. It bubbled and then solidified.
Calcium Hydroxide 1/2 tbsp. of polymer. It raised, then solidified.
Magnesium Sulfate 1/8 of a fl. oz. of polymer. It sank and broke apart.
Cobalt Chloride 1/4 tbsp. of polymer. It sank and turned pink.

Note: Because of the chemical amounts, we changed the amount of polymer.

Figure 9–5. (continued)

maintain our data and helped me assume a more active role than I ever had before. Our personalities shined through, even down to the day before we left, when we were packing our box to take with us. I remember the three boys putting our necessary supplies in the box and how upset I got because it was not organized enough. Perhaps it was my nervousness showing through, but concentrating my energy on getting ready for the conference helped ease my tension.

The day finally came for the conference. We put a lot of preparation into our presentation because we wanted our research to be taken seri-

Figure 9–6.   Polymer group's KIC presentation

ously by our fellow scientists. My whole class piled in a bus, along with
our posters, demonstrations, samples, and literature, to join more than
150 other students to share research, ask questions, and be inspired.
Despite the practice presentations, I was still very nervous, but I knew that
I was not up there on stage alone. As fate would have it, during the first
minute of our presentation, our box of materials fell off the table. The
team sprung into action and made a quick recovery. I think it actually
made us relax a little, and the rest of our presentation went very well. (See
Figure 9–6.) We had prepared small bags of sample everyday polymers for
the audience, and we learned that most people really didn't know how
common polymers are in the world around us. This generated a really
interesting discussion during the question-and-answer time. We received
many compliments from guests and fellow students on our presentation,
and Joey, Stewart, Chase, and I celebrated the success of our joint venture.

Aside from our own presentation, we thoroughly enjoyed attending
our fellow scientists' presentations and participating in the hands-on presentations. It was so fascinating to see so many different topics being
investigated in so many different ways. It was also a wonderful opportunity to spend a day talking with and learning from students from other
schools. We were able to enjoy lunch together, talk about our research,
and exchange contact information for future correspondence. We were
also treated to meeting science author Seymour Simon, the keynote
speaker. What a thrill to meet one of our very favorite authors, whose
many science books lined the chalk ledges and shelves in our classroom.
All in all, it was quite a remarkable day!

More than nine years have passed since that day, and I still remember KIC as one of the most rewarding experiences of my life. Now I try
to inspire others, just as Mrs. Hoyer inspired me. I continue to volunteer
each year to help budding young scientists investigate questions and

prepare for their presentations at KIC. I visit classrooms and correspond with students via the "Ask Meg" section of the KIC website and delight in meeting fellow KIC participants each year at KIC. Beyond KIC, I am now a college student at Juniata College majoring in chemistry (I guess the polymer interest really stuck!), and I am planning a career as a science educator. Not only did KIC meet my needs as a young scientist, but I gained confidence as a public speaker, overcame my shyness, learned how to be flexible and work with others, improved my organizational skills, and most of all, learned how to think outside the box. And that has made all the difference!

Epilogue to Meg's KIC Story: A Reunion of the Polymer Group

> In 1995, Chase, Meg, Joey, and Stewart collaborated to investigate the mysterious topic of polymers. Where are they now, and where has their scientific interest taken them? Ten years later, three of the members of the polymer group get together to recollect their experiences.

Seated at a table, looking through pictures and artifacts of their KIC experience, members of the polymer group begin to remember their adventure.

Chase recalls how their interest in polymers developed. "After Mr. Carico visited and introduced us to polymers, we looked it up in books and figured out that polymers were plastics. We noticed that all those recycling symbols that you see on the bottom of things were about polymers. Then my grandmother had this stuff that you could plant plants in, it was like a gel, and we were curious about that. . . . It just started to kind of snowball. We realized we [had] picked a topic that had a lot of possibilities."

Stewart remembers adventures in his kitchen one day after school when Megan visited. "I remember reading that once you make a polymer, you can break it down back into water by adding salt. I couldn't find any salt in the house, so we just used garlic salt and ended up making an awful stinky mess trying it out." They laugh.

Megan recalls experimenting in the school yard, attempting to work polymers into the classic baking-soda-and-vinegar volcano. "We'd added baking soda and vinegar together and it [erupted] and we tried to throw a polymer in there."

"Yeah, we thought we might be able to stop volcanoes with a polymer," Chase chimes in.

"Seriously, I think we thought that whole experiment was a little more realistic than it actually [was]. We did discover, though, that if we put the polymer in the vinegar, it gelled the vinegar and prevented the reaction from occurring," Megan says.

Figure 9–7.   Megan and Stewart, 2004 reunion

Figure 9–8.   Chase and Megan, 2004 reunion

But messy misadventures aren't all that KIC brings to mind ten years later.

All of these young adults can appreciate their choice of topic when they look back on it. "I think it's really cool that we did a project on polymers. . . . I didn't fully understand what polymers were until I got to high school," Stewart says.

"I was the same way," Meg agrees. She recalls learning about polymers in a high school advanced placement chemistry course. "My chemistry teacher started off by saying that none of us would have any clue what a polymer was, and I was like, 'Oh I do! I was doing this in the fourth grade!'"

"We had the gist of it," Stewart observes.

"We might not have understood all of the technical words, but we understood the basic concepts," Meg says.

"I think we had good ideas. We thought a lot about real applications," Meg muses. "We got to plan our investigations ourselves and we came out of it with a more authentic view of science . . . because you know, in the science world, scientists get to create ideas and spend time investigating them."

The atmosphere of KIC may be what they remember best. Chase recalls the excitement of the day of KIC: "It was fun for the day to feel like a scientist and feel important, to be able to present the stuff you'd been working on. . . . It felt very official and very cool."

Stewart also remembers the energy and feeling of the experience: "We did a whole project, a whole presentation on it, and it was so laid-back, it was so relaxed, and we had such a great time doing it. I think it was a good way to feed our natural curiosity."

For all of them, this natural curiosity is at the heart of science. Chase reflects, "I guess you always think that scientists need a degree. But now that I look back on it, even as a kids' inquiry participant, I was a scientist

Figure 9–9.   Megan and Joe, 2004 reunion

even then. I realize now that having a degree doesn't necessarily make you a scientist."

Stewart has a similar line of thought. "I think people have this idea that scientists always wear lab coats and work in laboratories and are a little crazy. But I think, at least through KIC, and through my personal experiences in college, all it takes to be a scientist is to have a love and a drive to figure out what's really happening."

Megan, too, thinks that the students at KIC are scientists by virtue of their curiosity. "They're curiosity driven and have great questions and do their own experiments and find out about the world." She continues, "I think that defines a scientist, so I consider them and myself a scientist, too."

Stewart mentions that his father is a professional scientist at Johns Hopkins. "He's told me a lot about his research and it seems that it sort of comes full circle. . . . His childlike curiosity is what still drives him at forty or fifty. He refers to being a scientist as, you know, being a kid. He talks about it with that look in his eyes, with all sorts of anxiety and excitement just to get to the lab and see if his results have worked out and [to] figure out what's happening. Just like we did. We couldn't wait for the next day to work on our investigation. We wanted to do something fun and we wanted to experiment and see what happened. That's what science is all about."

Where are these young scientists now? For all of these young people, science is a part of their lives, though they might not pursue careers as professional scientists. Chase is majoring in biology at the University of Maryland, Baltimore County, and plans to continue on to medical school. Meg is a sophomore majoring in chemistry at Juniata College in Pennsylvania and plans to pursue a career in teaching science to young students. Stewart is thinking about science also; as a student at Washington University in St. Louis, he's enjoyed courses in physics and continues to explore the possibilities. Joe is a sophomore at Salisbury State University in Maryland and hasn't yet decided on his career path.

10 The Nuts and Bolts of Organizing and Hosting KIC

As the previous chapters have illustrated, a year spent working toward KIC is quite different from classroom to classroom and year to year. Such is also the case with the conference itself. Past KICs have involved as few as two classes and as many as seven, with first-grade students through middle school students participating (although not at the same KIC). KICs have been single-school events and multiple-school gatherings with classes representing as many as six different school systems. College classrooms, elementary school auditoriums, outdoor classrooms, and even hotel meeting rooms have been the sites of KIC presentations. Each individual KIC is always unique, and they always will be because of the flexibility that allows, and encourages, each of you to tailor certain aspects of KIC to meet your own individual needs. While the underlying goals and principles of KIC are the same from year to year, you can customize the details to create your own version of the day of KIC.

What follows is a bit of information to help you to plan your KIC and some how-tos to guide you in making your KIC vision a KIC reality. We have organized the chapter into a KIC year from an organizational perspective and have relied upon our past experiences to provide guidance, suggestions, and some tools to help you organize and host your own Kids' Inquiry Conference.

Summer to Early September

Deciding What Type of KIC to Hold

When you begin thinking about organizing or hosting KIC, one of the first things you will need to decide upon is the type of KIC you want to have.

Single-school KICs are those in which all of the participants are from the same school.

Multi-school KICs have participants from two or more schools.

When making this decision, it is helpful to take into consideration the age group of the students involved. Successful KICs have included students as young as first grade and as old as high school, but not at the same time or in the same place. In general, it is recommended to delineate between primary (grades 1–2), intermediate (grades 3–5), middle school (grades 6–8), and high school (grades 9–12) when deciding on an age group for a specific KIC.

Deciding Where to Hold KIC

Once you have determined whether your KIC will be a single-school or multi-school event, you can decide upon a host location.

- Single-school KICs are generally held within the school facilities.
- Multi-school KICs might be held
  - at the facilities of one of the participating schools
  - at a local community college or university
  - at a local science-related business

Both types of KICs have the same basic space requirements:

- a common room large enough for all students to eat lunch at the same time
- a room with enough seating for everyone for the keynote address
- rooms for the presentations
- a welcome area for check-in and information
- a room, or other open space, for hands-on demonstrations and poster displays

When considering the suitability of possible locations, keep in mind the following suggestions:

- Your space should be in as compact an area as possible to facilitate movement among activities.
- One large common room can serve multiple purposes; the welcome area, the lunch area, hands-on displays, and the keynote address could all be located in a cafeteria or an auditorium.
- Classrooms work well for the presentation breakout sessions. The number of rooms needed will be dictated by the total number of presentations and attendees.

Deciding When to Hold KIC

KIC is generally held during a school day, usually a Tuesday, Wednesday, or Thursday, near the end of the school year to allow ample time for students to conduct their research. When deciding upon the date, day, and time of your KIC, consider the following:

- Make sure your space is available on the day you want to hold the conference.
- Check the school calendars of all participating classes. School responsibilities such as testing days and field trips need to be taken into account.
- Try to avoid scheduling on a Monday or the day after an off day to allow for last-minute in-class preparation.
- Schedule KIC so that there is time for follow-up. We suggest having it about three to four weeks before the end of the school year.
- When planning the time, you will need to take into account the participating schools' arrival and dismissal times to allow enough time for travel, when needed.
- In general, a five-hour time block plus travel time can accommodate a multi-school KIC. Less time may be needed for a single-school KIC, depending upon the number of participants.
- Participating teachers will need to know a start and end time early on to plan for buses and chaperones. However, final schedule adjustments can be made later in the year based on the number of student participants and other logistical considerations.

For more on scheduling, see "The KIC Schedule" later in this chapter.

Deciding What Elements of KIC to Include

Over the years, the day of KIC has grown and evolved into an event that includes various elements. Making decisions on what elements to include will help in planning the amount of time needed for the day.

Core Elements

Presentations

Presentations are the breakout sessions where student scientists share their research with an audience of their peers. These presentations are considered a major component of KIC.

- Concurrent sessions are generally composed of three to four individual or group presentations.
- Presentations are each allotted an equal amount of time.
- Each presentation includes time for introductions and question-and-answer periods.

Hands-on Displays

Hands-on displays offer student scientists the opportunity to share their research in a more informal and interactive way than the presentations. They are the second major component of KIC.

- Hands-on displays are made available to all attendees by scheduling them in a time period separate from the breakout sessions, such as during tours or lunch periods.

Optional Elements

Keynote Presentation

A keynote speaker is not a required KIC component, but it has almost always been a part of past KICs.

The keynote speech is usually

- approximately a half hour in duration
- scheduled at the end of the day's events, providing an opportunity for reflection on the KIC experience
- attended by all participants and visitors, enabling each group to gather together prior to departure
- about a kid-friendly topic, one that students would find interesting; insects and space are some of the more popular topics of past KIC keynotes

When choosing a keynote speaker, you might consider

- local celebrities with science connections or careers
- children's science authors
- university professors or graduate students with interesting research interests
- representatives from area zoos, aquariums, wildlife sanctuaries, or conservation centers
- high school student scientists
- science mentors
- a panel of people in science-related careers

Should you decide to invite a keynote speaker, encourage him or her to take part in all of the day's activities by visiting presentations and hands-on displays and interacting with the students. Often, the keynote speaker will share his or her excitement, reactions, and observations about KIC before focusing on the keynote talk.

Tours

Single-school KICs that hold a conference at their own site or multi-school KICs held at the site of one of the participating schools would not include a tour in their KIC planning. But for those of you who make the trip to a less familiar site, tours are worth thinking about. Tours might include

- a general tour of the facility or campus
- visits to working labs
- demonstrations by professors, scientists, or specialists
- brief visits with science professionals
- specially designed or featured exhibits

Site tours are generally planned by the contact at the host institution; however, be sure to include tour guides or monitors as you plan your job assignments for KIC.

Reading Room

The reading room is an area in which the latest, and best, of children's science trade books are made available for browsing. In the spirit of KIC, these books should be the best-quality science trade books. Some options for obtaining them include writing to publishers to request copies, featuring books from the school library, gathering a collection from the classroom libraries of participating teachers, or borrowing from local lending libraries.

Space requirements for the reading room include

- adequate room for readers to circulate among the books
- places to display the books
- chairs or other seating arrangements

You can schedule visits to the reading room

- during hands-on time
- in lieu of taking a tour
- after finishing lunch

Or you can include it as a more formal scheduled stop during the day.

You might also want to consider a review box where students can provide some feedback on the books they chose to read.

Goodie Bags

The distribution of goodie bags or giveaway items is not an essential piece of KIC but might be an idea that you would want to consider. Here are some suggestions if this is something you would like to do:

- Start soliciting for donations early in the year. Remember the fiscal year for businesses generally begins July 1, making the summer months an excellent time to ask for donations, since discretionary funds are still full!

- Ask for a quantity sufficient enough to ensure all students will get one of each item.

- Provide potential donors with some information about KIC and be sure to invite them to attend. (You could include the publicity announcement with your request for donations; see Appendix T, page 156.)

- Look for items with science connections or those with connections to the host institution.

Potential donors include

- publishers of children's science trade books or science magazines (e.g., bookmarks, posters, author profiles, or a free issue)

- local businesses

- your host institution

- national science organizations, especially those with education divisions

We suggest boxing up the goodie bags for each class and giving them to the teachers for classroom distribution. Don't forget to include one for the teacher!

Deciding Who Will Participate

If you are hosting KIC at your school, you probably have an idea of who will be participating. A great way to introduce KIC to fellow teachers is during a faculty meeting. However, if you are planning to hold KIC on a larger scale, and would like to invite teachers from different schools to attend, there are several ways to interest potential KIC participants:

- Contact the administration and faculty of neighboring schools to gauge interest.

- Inquire among coworkers and teachers within your school district.

- Call your district office and arrange for a newsletter posting or a systemwide mailing.

- If you are a member of an online community, use that resource to find potential participants.

When putting out your call for participants, whether it's during a faculty meeting or a more formal multi-school meeting, you will want to have some KIC information available to share. Refer interested parties to the KIC website and provide sample copies of *KIC Journals*, programs, and other materials for them to review. You may even want to schedule a KIC-Off to provide an opportunity for a more in-depth, hands-on exploration of KIC.

KIC-Off

Think of a KIC-Off as a workshop or meeting designed to provide enough information so that attendees can make an informed decision on whether or not they would like to participate in KIC.

Although KIC-Offs have varied slightly in terms of their structure, they all share some of the same features.

- Hands-on activities generally start the day to get attendees into the spirit of inquiry.

- KIC host staff and KIC alumni teachers share some of the history of KIC—how it first started and how it has evolved.

- Attendees are introduced to key KIC concepts and KIC alumni and staff share successful KIC strategies and tell KIC narratives.

- Visuals such as videos, photographs, and slide shows provide attendees with a glimpse of actual conferences. You can access a slideshow and photographs of a KIC by visiting *esiponline .learnserver.net/kic*.

- Resources, in the form of a *KIC Help Book*, are made available. This packet of materials contains general information about KIC and sample forms and templates that will be used for KIC.

Over the course of the meeting, attendees discuss the meaning of inquiry, ask questions, voice concerns, and share some of their classroom stories. For those who are new to planning a KIC, you will also likely spend time discussing the various elements and your KIC vision. At the end of the day's meeting, attendees leave with much food for thought. Ask them to consider whether they would like to be a part of KIC and give them a deadline by which they will need to commit to participation.

September to January

When organizing or hosting KIC, it is important to know that while KIC is a year-round classroom commitment, much of the organizational work is front- and back-ended. Much of the planning has to be completed at the start of the school year and much of the rest of the work cannot be completed until about a month before the day of KIC. Use the huge down period in between to attend to as many preconference details as possible.

Keeping in Contact

Establish a method of communication for KIC organizers and teachers who are participating in your KIC. You might consider

- regularly scheduled in-person meetings
- emails
- telephone conference calls
- website postings

After teachers have elected to participate in KIC, there are some things you can do to ensure that the group remains committed throughout the school year and returns the next school year:

- Put together and distribute a contact list to all participants.
- Provide resources and support for inquiry in the classroom. This can be as basic as providing a list of text and Internet resources or as involved as offering support in the classroom in an advisory capacity.

KIC Calendar of Events and Checklists

The KIC calendar serves as a reminder of what is due and when. We generally mark those dates when teachers will receive information from us as well as those deadlines by which they must submit information to us. In planning out the calendar we have found it helpful to work backward from the date of KIC to determine when to schedule deadlines.

Highlighted dates might include when various information will be distributed, such as

- chaperone letters
- instructions for moderators
- publicity announcements
- scheduling sign-up sheets

Deadlines might include when specific materials need to be submitted, such as

- signed permission forms
- presentation blurbs

- completed session sign-up sheets
- journal articles

Teachers and/or coordinators might also want to use their own individualized checklists for those dates that are specific to their own KIC responsibilities. We have constructed separate checklists that have, in the past, been used by teachers and coordinators. You may find these checklists helpful as is or you might choose to tailor them to meet your own particular needs. Sample checklists for hosts and teachers are provided in Appendices F and G, pages 141–42.

January to March

Applications to Present
Traditionally, students begin working on their applications to present in January and submit their applications early in February. If the host institution or planning committee will be involved in reviewing the applications, set up a procedure for the submission of applications. As stated previously (see Charles Pearce's discussion in Chapter 3), the applications are often reviewed by the classroom teacher. However, this is a decision you need to make with the teachers.

Firming Up Numbers
- Ask each teacher to provide the number of students he or she will bring to KIC.
- Ask each teacher to provide a rough estimate of how many presentations and hands-on displays he or she anticipates having. Although the number of presentations and hands-on displays will likely change before the actual day of KIC, an estimate is needed at this time to make certain that adequate facilities have been booked and to allow for additional space reservations.

KIC Schedule
How well you structure your KIC schedule will definitely go a long way toward coordinating and hosting a successful KIC. In fact, a carefully planned schedule is one of the most important tasks that a coordinator will undertake. To begin mapping out your schedule, answer the following questions.

- What elements of KIC make up your version of KIC?
- If you are having hands-on presentations, do you need one session or more? Consider the number of participants as well as the size of

the rooms to determine whether you will be best served by separate sessions.

- What time will your classes be able to arrive at the KIC location?
- What time will your classes have to leave the KIC location?
- How many breakout presentation and hands-on sessions do you have scheduled?

The answers to these questions will determine when KIC can begin and when it must end. They will also determine how much time you have left to allot for lunch, the keynote speech, welcoming remarks, and movement between sessions. To show our thought and planning process, we offer the following information about our 2003 KIC.

- Our six classes could arrive between 9:30 and 9:45.
- All of our classes had to leave before 2:45.
- We wanted our keynote speech to last a half hour.
- We needed to reserve a half-hour period lunch.
- Our elements included a guided tour of the host university (offered twice to accommodate the entire group), a reading room, presentations, and two hands-on sessions.
- We needed to accommodate all of the presentations.
- We needed to incorporate traveling time because we were moving between buildings.
- We needed time for welcoming remarks.

Knowing all of this, we began plotting out our schedule. We decided to begin KIC at 10:00 and end it at 2:30 to accommodate everyone's arrival and departure needs. That gave us a total of four and a half hours to work with.

- Of those four and a half hours, we needed a half hour for lunch and a half hour for the keynote. (Three and a half hours remained.)
- Given the large number of presentations and attendees, we needed to schedule half of the students to take tours at the same time that the other half would be with the hands-on displays. Groups would then switch. The tour–hands-on combination would be scheduled twice, and each would last 20 minutes each. (Two hours and fifty minutes remained.)
- We needed to set aside time for a restroom break and packing. We set aside ten minutes immediately before the keynote speech. (Two hours and forty minutes remained.)

- We scheduled ten minutes for opening remarks. (Two hours and thirty minutes remained.)
- A large number of presentations dictated that we would need four individual sessions.
  - Each session would have five breakout rooms.
  - Each of the breakout rooms would have three presentations.
  - Each session would need to last thirty minutes, for a total of two hours. (Thirty minutes remained.)
- Time still needed to be allotted for movement between buildings and rooms, which would occur six times during the day. We allotted five minutes for each transition. The entire KIC day was accounted for. (See Figure 10–1.)

Kids' Inquiry Conference Schedule

Location:	University of Maryland, Baltimore County University Center: Ballroom, Ballroom Lounge, and Adjacent Classrooms Academic IV Building, Rooms 207, 208, and 210
9:30–9:50	Students arrive at UMBC. Presenters bring materials to their assigned rooms. Students pick up name tags and programs at check-in.
10:00–10:10	Opening remarks
10:10–10:40	Session 1
10:45–11:15	Session 2
11:20–11:40	Tour 1 and Hands-On 1
11:45–12:15	Lunch
12:20–12:40	Tour 2 and Hands-On 2
12:45–1:15	Session 3
1:20–1:50	Session 4
1:50–2:00	Restroom break Students pack up materials.
2:00–2:30	Keynote Speaker, Don Robinson-Boonstra, NASA (in the Ballroom)
2:30	Dismissal Certificates, giveaways, and *KIC Journals* distributed.

Figure 10–1. Sample KIC schedule

Use your answers to the questions at the beginning of this section to guide you through a process similar to the one we used to arrive at our final schedule for KIC 2003.

Deciding Upon KIC Personnel

To make certain that your KIC runs smoothly, you will have to enlist the aid of others besides the teachers of the participating classes. The number of people who are needed, and the specific roles that must be filled, will vary depending upon whether you are having a single-school KIC or multi-school KIC. The host location will also be a factor. When soliciting for volunteers, be certain to (1) explain that there are a number of roles that need to be filled, (2) provide a short description of the types of tasks that need to be done, and (3) give people a choice as to how they would like to help.

- Single-school KICs must have moderators.
- Multi-school KICs must have moderators, chaperones, greeters, and welcome table personnel.

Other personnel may be added in both instances to meet the needs of individual KICs.

Moderators are needed for each breakout session. They will

- welcome the presenters
- help presenters set up and assist with unexpected situations, such as unfamiliar equipment and spills
- introduce the presenters
- facilitate question-and-answer periods
- keep the session on schedule

Provide the moderators with a list of their responsibilities in advance. (See Appendix L, page 148, for a sample.)

Chaperones normally arrive with each class in varying numbers.

- They generally are assigned duties by their respective teachers.
- They can serve as additional eyes and ears.

Send copies of the chaperone letter (see Appendix E, page 140, for a sample) to participating teachers so that they can give the letter to chaperones before the day of the conference.

Greeters await the arrival of the classes and take them to the welcoming area. It is a good idea to have at least two greeters per arriving class. Their duties include

- delivering the class to the welcome table
- walking presenters to their session rooms
- helping with session setup needs
- answering questions
- helping out at the welcome table, when needed

Throughout the day, the greeters can be assigned various duties.

Welcome table personnel are needed to distribute name tags, programs, and other handouts. Have at least two people manning the table, and increase welcome table personnel as the number of participants increases. After each student receives his or her items, the volunteers at the welcome table direct the students to the location selected for welcoming remarks. If this is a distance from the welcome table, the greeters should escort the groups.

You might want to assign a *photographer* and/or a *videographer* so that you will have a visual record of the day.

When planning for workers and duties, consider the following:

- One person should always be available to troubleshoot. This is generally the coordinator.
- Some of these duties can be performed by the same people. For example, your greeters might also be your photographers. Generally, moderators should not be assigned other duties, as they need to be available to presenters.
- Think about creating a chart of job assignments and distributing it to all volunteers so they can easily identify where they should be, and what they should be doing, at any given point in the day.

April to May

As the day of the conference approaches, coordinators of all versions of KIC will need to complete many of the same tasks. Some of these, such as the publicity announcements, are stand-alone tasks, while others are dependent upon each other and must be completed in a logical order. For example, you cannot create the KIC program or schedule until the session assignments have been completed. The session sign-up sheets must be completed before you can do the name tags. The order of tasks, and the reasoning behind it, will become a bit clearer after you read the next few pages.

Communicating Preparation Instructions and Deadlines

In order for the logistics team to make final preparations for KIC, certain information needs to be provided by the classroom teachers in April. It may be helpful at this time to send an email or letter stating the information needed and deadlines for transmission of the information. The following information will be needed:

1. A class list with the teacher's name, the school, and students' first and last names. It is also helpful to identify on the class list which students are presenters and which students are participating in hands-on demonstrations.

2. A list of presentations with the title of each presentation, group members' names, the advertising blurb (for more on blurbs, see page 51), and the teacher's name for easy identification.

3. A list of hands-on demonstrations with the title and group members' names for each.

4. A list of audiovisual needs for presentations so that equipment can be reserved.

5. A list of any special accommodations needed for students.

Publicity Announcements

If you decide that you would like to make your students' accomplishments public, you should consider sending out publicity announcements to the local newspapers for all participating schools. These announcements are also handy for keeping administrators and parents informed. Publicity announcements should be distributed about one month prior to the day of KIC. When putting together your announcements, include the following:

- date and time
- location
- participant information (teachers' names, schools, grades, school systems)
- a brief description of KIC
- coordinator or host contact information

A sample publicity announcement can be found in Appendix T, page 156. Be certain to include a short cover letter with an invitation to attend.

Permission Slips

Most schools have their own specific guidelines for permission forms for field trips. However, an additional permission form may be needed related to photographs, videos, and websites, depending upon your plans for documenting and sharing images of KIC with a wider audience. Consult with school personnel and district offices about policies and required permission.

Planning Presentation Sessions and Audience Sign-Up

Whether you hold a single-school KIC or a multi-school KIC, you need to plan out your session presentations. Presenters are assigned to a specific session in advance of KIC and a presentation schedule is created. The presentation schedule is distributed to classes in advance so that students can indicate which sessions they would like to attend. These preferences and the number of participants help determine the audience assignments.

In order to assign presentations to specific sessions, consider the following:

- Each thirty-minute session is generally composed of three related presentations (allot ten minutes for each presentation).
- Review all the presentation blurbs and look for common denominators. For example, there may be several presentations about bacteria and several that have to do with consumer testing.
- Once you sort the blurbs by topics, take into consideration the groups. If possible, try to mix and match the groups so that different classes are represented in each session.
- Once you have all the blurbs separated into groups of three, count the sets to verify that you have allocated enough rooms and enough sessions to accommodate your needs. For example, if you have five presentation rooms, you can accommodate fifteen presentations per each thirty-minute session (three presentations times five rooms). If you have scheduled four session times throughout the day using those five rooms each time, you can accommodate a total of sixty presentations.
- Instead of using room numbers, we assign colors to the presentation rooms to facilitate name-tag coding and eliminate confusion with regard to room numbers. So, for Sessions 1, 2, 3, and 4, groups of presentations are assigned to the blue, green, red, orange, and yellow rooms.

Sign-Up Sheets

Once room assignments have been completed, we use the blurbs to create audience sign-up sheets for each session (see Figures 10–2 and 10–3 for sample sign-up instructions and a session sign-up sheet). Then we send the sheets to each class and students sign up for the sessions they wish to attend. In order to ensure that the audience for each session is balanced between the classes, we allocate each class a maximum number of spots for each session. Presenters for any given session are included as part of the audience count for each class.

This procedure is much less complicated than it might sound and is one that we have instituted for several reasons:

1. It gives the students choices about which presentations they will attend.

2. By placing a limit on the number of students from one class that can attend any given presentation session, we bring about a balanced mingling of classes.

The Kids' Inquiry Conference

Sign-Up Instructions

Provided are the sign-up sheets for KIC at [insert location]. Please have each student sign up for ONE space during each session.

(Please have students print their names so that it is less likely that spelling errors will be made on their name tags.)

A. Sign-up sheets include

Session 1—Red, Blue, Green, Yellow, Orange
Session 2—Red, Blue, Green, Yellow, Orange
Session 3—Red, Blue, Green, Yellow, Orange
Session 4—Red, Blue, Green, Yellow, Orange

Spaces are limited to provide a mix of schools in each presentation room. Please do not add any additional spaces to the sign-up sheets.

B. Make sure student *presenters* sign up for the session and location where they will be presenting.

C. **Sign-up sheets must be returned by [insert date] evening, via fax or dropped off or emailed, so that we can prepare the name tags.**

D. Questions???? Call or email [insert contact name]: [insert phone number] or [insert email address]

Thank you! We look forward to seeing you at KIC!

Figure 10–2.   Sample sign-up instructions

3. The use of limited slots allows us to make certain that each of the presentations is well attended but does not exceed the seating capacity.

4. Assigning students to specific sessions enables teachers to know where their students are at all times.

Remember, you do not have to follow this particular plan. This is only one example of how you might structure your presentation sessions.

Name Tags

For those of you who decide to hold a single-school KIC, name tags will probably not be a major concern. But for those who participate in multischool KICs, especially those held at a neutral location, we suggest the use of name tags to identify students, the school they attend, and the sessions in which they will participate.

Name tags might be fashioned from two-by-four-inch labels printed on the computer or they might be handwritten on stick-on name tags. The information on the name tags can be as simple as the child's name or can include the following:

- the event name: the Kids' Inquiry Conference
- the date of KIC
- the location of KIC
- the student's name
- the school or teacher's name
- the sessions the student will attend

Consider using different color-coding systems to

- differentiate one school from another
- map out students' session selections

Color-coded labels are useful for several reasons:

1. They remind students of what room they should be in for each session.

2. KIC personnel can simply look at the name tags to get students to the proper destination.

3. Sign-ups for individual sessions are limited by seating capacity. The name tags prevent attendees from session jumping, thereby ensuring that each presentation has an audience equal to that in other rooms.

KIC '03

UMBC
May 28, 2003

Session I
Red Room

Can we build a faster car?

By Chris Jones and Monica Hayes
Come see the fastest car at KIC . . .
Zoom, zoom, zoom!!

Magnet Wars!

By Shannon O'Donnell
Electromagnets versus regular magnets—
which is strongest?

An Electrifying Experience

By Joshua Witter
Come see the fascinating world of computers and how they work.
I created a computer circuit board from scratch.
Find out what I have learned.

1. _____
2. _____
3. _____
4. _____
5. _____
6. _____
7. _____
8. _____
9. _____

Figure 10–3.   Sample session sign-up sheet

Certificates of Participation

In keeping with the noncompetitive philosophy of KIC, we don't give any awards. Instead, we present all student attendees with a certificate of participation, whether they are presenters, hands-on demonstrators, or audience members. Use the class lists provided by the teachers to personalize the certificates. Because of time limitations, we give the certificates to KIC teachers for distribution upon return to their classrooms. (A sample certificate is provided in Appendix D, page 139.)

Journal Articles

Journal articles are a staple of all kinds of KICs. Each presenter or group of presenters writes a journal article about the research. Each of these articles is then assembled into a *KIC Journal*. (For more information on *KIC Journal*s, see page 51.)

KIC Journals

- are compiled for each KIC
- publish the students' work as submitted (editing should be done by the individual teachers prior to submission of the articles)
- usually are printed on $8\frac{1}{2}$-by-11-inch paper with a cardstock cover and assembled with a binding machine to create a finished look

Assembly of the journals can be simplified by clarifying the journal submission requirements:

- Set a deadline for submission that allows ample time for copying and assembly.
- Have journal articles sent by email or given to you on a disk so that copies are clean.
- Agree upon a software program, such as Microsoft Word, that must be used for writing all articles.

Decide whether you will provide each student with his or her own copy of the journal on the day of the conference or if you will provide master copies to the participating teachers, who can then make copies for their students.

Sample *KIC Journal* articles may be accessed at the KIC website, *esiponline.learnserver.net/kic*.

Signs

Even if KIC is held at your own facility, it is a good idea to post signs designating the specific areas being used for the conference. Signs are vital, however, when the event is being held at a neutral location. The signs do not have to be elaborate. We generally use a combination of copy paper, poster board, and construction paper to put ours together. The signs can be constructed as soon as your scheduling of sessions has been completed. We save ours from year to year, whenever possible, to save ourselves a bit of time.

Use signs to

- indicate where visitors should park
- direct visitors from the parking area to the welcome area
- designate the reading room, the general meeting area, and the meeting spot for the tours, if these are features of your KIC
- mark the areas where individual classes will place their belongings
- distinguish between the various presentation rooms (We match the paper color of the sign to the color that we've use to code the room.)
- point out the hands-on display area

If you are moving between buildings, place directional signs on the inside and outside of the entrance doors to facilitate movement. Do a trial run with your signs to see if there are any areas where you need to provide additional direction.

KIC Program

We always provide a KIC program for all participants and attendees. It not only serves as a guide for the day's events but also becomes a memento for participants. Although the creation of the program itself is not time-consuming, make certain to allow ample time for copying and folding the programs. Keep this in mind when setting a deadline for determining presentation assignments. Allow enough time between assigning students to sessions and KIC to prepare the programs. The programs need not be anything fancy. We use $8\frac{1}{2}$-by-11-inch paper, folded lengthwise. The text is formatted in Microsoft Word, but any word-processing program would work as well.

Program elements include

- a title page that includes the date and place of the conference
- a short biography of your keynote speaker (A picture can also be included if one is available.)
- some brief information about KIC for those who may not be familiar with it

- the day's schedule, including the times and places of presentations as well as the names of presenters and their presentation titles (Your KIC schedule and session sign-ups will provide you with all the information needed.)

- a thank-you to all who have provided assistance (List their names.)

- a blank page or two for notes

The Day of KIC

Workers' Meeting

On the day of KIC, schedule a workers meeting one hour before your attendees are scheduled to arrive. Use this meeting to

- make certain that all of your volunteers are present
- distribute copies of duty assignments and confirm assignments
- answer any questions and address any concerns
- assign preconference tasks to ready the conference site

Readying the Site

Although you should try to do as much conference preparation as possible before the day of the event, there are some things that just might have to be done in the time immediately preceding KIC. This is particularly true when KIC will be held at a neutral location. After your workers meeting, have your volunteers do the following, as needed:

- Make certain that all presentation rooms are in order.
- Check equipment to make sure it is functioning correctly.
- If you are having a reading room, set up the books.
- At the welcome table, lay out all of the items to be distributed. Arrange name tags alphabetically by class.
- Put up all directional and parking signs.
- Designate lunch and storage areas for each class by hanging teacher designation signs.
- Hang the color-coded signs in areas directly outside of the rooms.
- Place any items for teachers in designated areas. (Items might include certificates, goodie bags, surveys, and journals.)

These last-minute tasks will vary according to the location and the elements of your KIC. When KIC is being held at a school, you will probably be able to have everything readied the evening before the conference. When KIC is being held at a neutral location, some additional tasks include

- checking parking regulations and confirming arrangements with facility managers
- providing participating teachers with driving directions and a map of the facility, if possible

Getting Started and Keeping It Going

Once the site has been readied and any last-minute details have been taken care of, your volunteers should be in their places, ready to perform their assigned duties.

Moderators need to be in their assigned presentation rooms before the presenters begin arriving so that they can

- greet the presenters
- ask students for their biographical data sheets to be used in the introductions (see page 53)
- help presenters arrange their equipment and/or materials
- demonstrate how any audiovisual equipment works
- ensure that the students are escorted back to the welcoming area

Greeters should be outside of the building, watching for arrivals. Between arrival and the welcoming remarks, the greeters will be almost constantly moving, shuttling students to and from presentation rooms and being available for the teachers, as needed. Only presenters will go to the presentation rooms; the others will first stow their lunches and other belongings and then be seated in the large common room. Once all attendees have been seated in the common room, the event begins.

A carefully constructed schedule will practically ensure that the day will run smoothly and on schedule. When the moderators keep the presentations on schedule and movement to and fro is kept within its designated timeframe, you will find that you need only monitor activity and ensure that everyone gathers on time for the keynote speaker.

Scheduling your keynote speaker as the last feature of the day helps facilitate a more orderly and timely departure for attendees.

- All attendees will be in the same place, with entire classes assembled in one seating area.

- Once the speech is completed, classes might be dismissed one at a time according to their bus pickup schedules.

- Belongings can be stored in the main meeting room for ease of gathering.

After all attendees have gone, it takes only a few moments to gather up the remaining items from the welcome table, check all rooms for any forgotten items, pack up the reading room books, and take down the directional signs. If you have elected to hold KIC at a neutral location, cleanup will probably be included in any facility fee or arrangements you have made. However, if KIC is being held in your school, you may want to make arrangements in advance with your custodian to have him or her clean up after the conference, or you might want to include a cleanup crew in your personnel list.

After KIC

For those who have coordinated or hosted KIC, the time after KIC is a period of reflection. While the day's events are still fresh in your mind, you can remember what worked and what did not. You can think about what might be changed the following year to make the conference even better. Consider gathering additional feedback in the following ways:

- Encourage attendees to provide feedback by distributing survey sheets.

  - Distribute *parent survey forms* to adult visitors and have the surveys returned to a specified location before the close of the conference. (See Appendix N, page 150, for sample.)

  - Provide teachers with *student survey forms* to be completed in class and returned to the KIC hosts or coordinators. (See Appendix O, page 151, for samples.)

- Hold a brief *post-KIC meeting* with all volunteers immediately after KIC so that they might share their thoughts about the day's successes, report any problems or concerns, and suggest changes for the future.

When you have your group meeting and later read the surveys, you are already starting to think about, and plan, your next KIC. The new KIC year is under way!

In Conclusion

Throughout this chapter we have tried to provide you with some general, and specific, information to help you to plan and organize your own KIC. Depending on what your version of KIC turns out to be, some of these tools and guidelines will be more helpful than others. Just as we have made changes from one KIC year to another, we anticipate that KIC will continue to evolve in the future. We suggest that you regularly stop by the KIC website for updates to keep abreast of KIC. We would love to hear from those of you who do decide to host KIC. We are also available to help you with any questions you might have. Visit the Elementary Science Integration Projects website at *www.esiponline.org* to contact us.

11 *Resources*

Throughout the KIC year, teachers gather various kinds of items—books, websites, materials, experts—all with the intent of sustaining and supporting their students' inquiry. To assist you in your search for resources, we suggest the following.

The KIC Website

The KIC website has been created and is maintained as a resource for KIC participants and their teachers. Features include

- "The KIC Gallery," a section that contains a slide show of a typical day at KIC, KIC photo albums, KIC artwork, and reflection pieces
- "Ask Meg," a section where former KIC participant Megan Dieckman shares her KIC expertise by fielding questions from the latest crop of KIC participants
- "Just for Kids," a section that contains annotated bibliographies of student-recommended books and websites
- "Just for Teachers," a section with KIC forms from the *KIC Help Book* and annotated bibliographies of videos, books, and Internet resources
- Sample *KIC Journal* articles of KIC participants, from 1994 to the present

  To visit the KIC website, go to *esiponline.learnserver.net/kic*.

The Elementary Science Integration Projects' Website

The Elementary Science Integration Projects (ESIP) promotes connections between language arts instruction and inquiry-based science in grades K–8. Project staff maintain a website for use by program participants and others who are interested in ESIP's work. The ESIP website, *www.esiponline.org*, is organized into three sections.

- In "About ESIP," visitors can read about the program's history, meet ESIP staff, and keep current on ESIP's publications and products.
- In "Books & Beyond," the focus goes beyond trade book basics to include information about selecting and evaluating books, articles on cutting-edge issues in children's books, connections between books and technology, and bibliographies of recommended science trade books.
- The basics of inquiry, literacy, and the standards are part of the "Classroom Connections" section. Other features include science-literacy connections, professional resources, and instructional strategies and activities related to inquiry, reading, and writing.

There are sections on the ESIP website that will be of particular interest to those participating in a KIC.

- In "Books and Beyond," a section called "Books Galore" contains bibliographies of science trade books sorted by unit of study, thematic focus, and author. Current bibliographies include books on life cycles, buildings and structures, plants, rocks and minerals, weather, flight, the seasons, and books by Jean Craighead George, Seymour Simon, Jim Arnosky, and Gail Gibbons, and more bibliographies are to follow.
- The "Bibliographies of Professional Resources for Educators" section includes a bibliography that is devoted to an exploration of science and literacy connections and another that is centered on nonfiction read-alouds.
- In "Classroom Connections," "Scientist's Notebooks" focuses on one particular way for students to keep records of inquiry. Directions are provided for constructing, using, and organizing science notebooks.
- In "Classroom Connections," "Kids' Classroom Research" addresses science questions: where they come from, how to inspire them, and how to investigate them. The section also offers suggestions on gathering research information, including preparing for note taking, note-taking strategies, ideas about organizing information, and presentation and publication ideas for sharing research.

Search It! Science

Search It! Science, an online searchable database of more than forty-five hundred highly recommended and regarded science-related trade books, is a product of the Elementary Science Integration Projects funded through a grant from the National Science Foundation. The database was created to serve as a reader advisory for a wide range of users including teachers, students, parents, and librarians. The database's design allows users to customize their search for titles based on their own particular needs and concerns. Bibliographies can be constructed based on subject, author, keywords, series, genre, reading level, awards, publisher, publication date, style of writing, or a combination of these and other search criteria. Cover scans, summaries, and reviews offer additional details about each book. *Search It! Science* is available on a subscription basis. To learn more about *Search It!* and to try a demo, go to *searchit.heinemann.com.*

Books

Science-related trade books are integral parts of every KIC classroom and have often been the origin of KIC questions and inquiry topics. Through reader-text interactions, students not only learn about the nature of science but also become familiar with scientists and the different ways that scientists go about their work. The following list of books presents an overall look at the work of particular scientists in the field. The list of books about the scientific process focuses on various processes of science such as observation, the importance of scientific drawing, problem solving, and record keeping. When used together in a classroom, books such as those on these two lists help students understand what it means to think, and work, like scientists.

Books About Scientists and Their Work

Batten, Mary. 2001. *Anthropologist: Scientist of the People.* Boston: Houghton Mifflin.
>   Anthropologist Magdalena Hurtado has spent years studying the Aché, a society of hunter-gatherers who live in the forests of Paraguay.

Jackson, Donna M. 1996. *The Bone Detectives: How Forensic Anthropologists Solve Crimes and Uncover Mysteries of the Dead.* Boston: Little, Brown.
>   Forensic anthropologists, such as Dr. Michael Charney, examine bones for clues to help police solve crimes.

Jackson, Ellen. 2002. *Looking for Life in the Universe: The Search for Extraterrestrial Intelligence.* Boston: Houghton Mifflin.
>   Along with her fellow scientists, astrophysicist Jill Tarter monitors outer space for signs that intelligent life-forms exist on other planets.

Kramer, Stephen. 2001. *Hidden Worlds: Looking Through a Scientist's Microscope.* Boston: Houghton Mifflin.
>   Microscopist Dennis Kunkel employs various types of microscopes to investigate objects that are often invisible to the naked eye.

Kress, Stephen W. 1997. *Project Puffin: How We Brought Puffins Back to Egg Rock.* Gardiner, ME: Tilbury House.

continued

Wildlife scientist Stephen Kress and fellow scientists and naturalists reintroduce puffins to tiny Eastern Egg Rock, an island along the coast of Maine.

Lasky, Kathryn. 2001. *Interrupted Journey: Saving Endangered Sea Turtles*. Cambridge, MA: Candlewick.
The combined efforts of volunteers, technicians, and veterinarians are directed toward saving endangered Kemp's ridley turtles.

Lehn, Barbara. 1998. *What Is a Scientist?* Brookfield, CT: Millbrook.
First-grade teacher Barbara Lehn presents young student scientists who think and work like scientists.

Martin, Jacqueline Briggs. 1998. *Snowflake Bentley*. Boston: Houghton Mifflin.
This biography of Wilson Bentley recounts the lifework of the Vermont farmer who became known for his photographic studies of snowflakes.

Norrell, Mark A., and Lowell Dingus. 1999. *A Nest of Dinosaurs: The Story of Oviraptor*. New York: Random House.
Paleontologists Mark Norell and Lowell Dingus journey to the Gobi Desert of Mongolia in search of fossils.

Osborn, Elinor. 2002. *Project UltraSwan*. Boston: Houghton Mifflin.
Biologists in the Trumpeter Swan Migration Project attempt to teach migratory routes to trumpet swans and reintroduce them to the northeastern coast of the United States.

Salmansohn, Pete, and Stephen W. Kress. 2002. *Saving Birds: Heroes Around the World*. Gardiner, ME: Tilbury House.
Dedicated people in New Zealand, Mexico, Malaysia, China, Israel, and the United States attempt to keep six different types of wild birds from becoming extinct.

Sayre, April Pulley. 2002. *Secrets of Sound: Studying the Calls and Songs of Whales, Elephants, and Birds*. Boston: Houghton Mifflin.
The efforts of acoustic biologists Christopher Clark, Katy Payne, and Bill Barklow are presented in this book about animal communications.

Swinburne, Stephen R. 2002. *The Woods Scientist*. Boston: Houghton Mifflin.
In the woods of northern Vermont, forester Sue Morse tracks animals as a means of learning more about the wildlife who make their home there.

Books About Scientific Processes

Allen, Marjorie N., and Shelley Rotner. 1991. *Changes*. New York: Macmillan.

> Side-by-side color photographs invite careful observation and comparison of the changes that nature undergoes.

Arnosky, Jim. 1988. *Sketching Outdoors in Winter.* New York: Lothrop, Lee and Shepard.

> Arnosky presents sketches of the outdoors that he drew in the New England winter weather and he shares his observations and strategies for producing the best sketches possible in spite of the challenges posed by the weather. (Also by the author: *Sketching Outdoors in Autumn* [1988] New York: Lothrop, Lee and Shepard; *Sketching Outdoors in Spring* [1987] New York: Lothrop, Lee and Shepard; and *Sketching Outdoors in Summer* [1988] Lothrop, Lee and Shepard.)

———. 2002. *Field Trips: Bug Hunting, Animal Tracking, Bird-Watching, and Shore Walking with Jim Arnosky*. New York: HarperCollins.

> Naturalist Jim Arnosky draws upon his own observations and experiences to share some tips for budding bug hunters, animal trackers, bird-watchers, and shore walkers.

Cole, Henry. 1998. *I Took a Walk*. New York: William Morrow.

> Fold-out illustrations of natural settings invite readers to carefully examine the woods, the meadow, the stream, and the pond to see what might be seen and heard while taking a walk at each of these spots. (Also by the author: *On the Way to the Beach* [2003] New York: Greenwillow.)

Dewey, Jennifer Owings. 2001. *Antarctic Journal: Four Months at the Bottom of the World*. New York: HarperCollins.

> Journal entries, letters sent home, photographs, and sketches provide a detailed look at Antarctica as seen, and experienced, by author-illustrator Dewey during her four-month stay.

Esbensen, Barbara Juster. 1996. *Echoes for the Eye: Poems to Celebrate Patterns in Nature*. New York: HarperCollins.

> Poetic text introduces and explores various recurring patterns that can be seen in nature if you know how to look for them.

Hoban, Tana. 1997. *Look Book*. New York: William Morrow.

> Look through the cutout portion of the page to view a small section of a photograph. Use your observation skills to guess what

continued

you're looking at, then turn the page to see how well developed your observation skills might be.

Minor, Wendell. 1998. *Grand Canyon: Exploring a Natural Wonder.* New York: Scholastic.
Artist Wendell Minor records his impressions of the Grand Canyon in his sketches and paintings, which he shares with readers along with his personal observations and reflections.

Pratt-Serafini, Joy. 2001. *Salamander Rain: A Lake and Pond Journal.* Nevada City, CA: Dawn.
This colorful lake and pond journal has a scrapbook-layout look to it with its detailed borders, journaling inserts, captions, note cards, articles, and fact boxes. (Also by the author: *Saguaro Moon* [2002] Nevada City, CA: Dawn.)

Rotner, Shelley, and Ken Kreisler. 1992. *Nature Spy.* New York: Macmillan.
What does it take to be a nature spy? To start with, it takes curiosity and a keen eye "to take a really close look, even closer and closer." Things look quite different when examined closely, as the book's photographs illustrate.

Rotner, Shelley, and Richard Olivo. 1997. *Close, Closer, Closest.* New York: Simon and Schuster Children's.
Linked sets of photographs zoom in on natural objects from three different distances to illustrate perspective and scale.

Sayre, April Pulley. 1997. *Put on Some Antlers and Walk Like a Moose: How Scientists Find, Follow, and Study Wild Animals.* New York: Henry Holt.
This look at the work of field scientists will help readers develop their own "animal-finding skills." The book also stresses the skills and procedures used to identify, count, measure, weigh, code, gather information, and record data about what you find.

Schaefer, Lola M. 2002. *What's Up, What's Down?* New York: HarperCollins.
Look up! What do you see? Look down! What do you see? This book shows that what you see depends on the perspective you take when looking.

continued

Selsam, Millicent Ellis. 1995. *How to Be a Nature Detective*. New York: HarperCollins.
A nature detective is a person who looks for clues to find answers to questions about nature. Questions relating to various animal tracks are posed to readers to help them reason which animals have been where.

Showers, Paul. 1991. *The Listening Walk*. New York: HarperCollins.
There are many things to see in nature, but have you ever thought about how much there is to hear? When the young girl in this book goes on a listening walk, she hears many different sounds, but as the character advises, you "don't have to take a walk to hear sounds . . . all you have to do is keep still and listen to them."

Swinburne, Stephen R. 1998. *Lots and Lots of Zebra Stripes: Patterns in Nature*. Honesdale, PA: Boyds Mills.
Patterns in nature are explored by way of exquisite color photographs in this photo-essay that will have readers searching for patterns in the world around them.

Talbott, Hudson. 2003. *Safari Journal*. New York: Harcourt.
This often humorous fictional journal account, which is based on the author's real-life travels, is fact packed and features diagrams, labeling, photographs, drawings, and examples of note taking.

Webb, Sophie. 2000. *My Season with Penguins: An Antarctic Journal*. Boston: Houghton Mifflin.
Journal writing and drawings document the facts, observations, and experiences of the author during her two-month stay studying the Adélie penguins in Antarctica.

Wright-Frierson, Virginia. 1996. *A Desert Scrapbook: Dawn to Dusk in the Sonoran Desert*. New York: Simon and Schuster Children's.
Author-artist Virginia Wright-Frierson shares some information, observations, notes, sketches, and reflections from her time watching and listening to the sights and sounds of the Sonoran Desert. (Also by the author: *An Island Scrapbook: Dawn to Dusk on a Barrier Island* [1998] New York: Simon and Schuster Children's and *A North American Rain Forest Scrapbook* [1999] New York: Walker.)

Websites

There are many excellent science-related websites that may be helpful to students for their research and to teachers for instruction on using Web resources in the classroom. The following list provides a sampling of some of the websites available. As with most print materials, information on the Web can be accurate, up-to-date, and well written, or it can be quite misleading and downright awful in terms of writing quality. For a further discussion about evaluating Internet resources for classroom research, go to *esiponline.org/classroom/implement/evaluating.html*.

General Science-Related Websites

The following websites will be excellent starting points for your students. These dependable sites cover a range of topics that have proven popular with past KIC student scientists.

Consumer Reports Online for Kids
www.zillions.org
>   Although this *Zillions* site is no longer adding new information, what is already there is an informative look at consumer testing, complete with examples and suggestions.

eNature.com
www.enature.com
>   This site contains online field guides from the National Audubon Society that focus on more than forty-eight hundred species of reptiles, insects, wildflowers, trees, amphibians, native plants, birds, butterflies, fish, mammals, seashells, seashore creatures, and spiders.

The Exploratorium
www.exploratorium.edu
>   With a wide range of features, including live webcasts, sports and science connections, the science of cooking, online exhibits, and hands-on activities, there is something on this site for every interest.

Virtual Field Trips Site
www.field-trips.org
>   On this site, more than forty virtual field trips, many of which are science related, are packed with information and colorful photographs.

continued

HowStuffWorks

www.howstuffworks.com

> For your KIC students who are interested in learning about what makes things tick, recommend this site, where they can learn how just about everything works.

Inventors and Inventions for K–12 Education

falcon.jmu.edu/~ramseyil/inventors.htm

> Your budding inventors might want to take a few moments to check out some of the websites devoted to famous inventors listed on this site or learn about resources for young inventors, like themselves.

KidsGardening

www.kidsgardening.com

> Although this website is designed primarily with teachers in mind, there is still plenty of information to pass along to young gardeners or plant researchers.

The Weather Channel

www.weather.com

> This website, with its top weather stories and daily videos, is a good starting point for students whose KIC questions relate to the weather.

Science Catalogs

As students research the work that scientists do, it's important that they have access to the tools and materials of scientists as well. Many teachers ask students to request funding in order to purchase some of the more specialized materials. As Charles Pearce notes in Chapter 3, "As the students seek sources for funding, they come to understand another aspect of being a scientist: finding money to continue their research." To assist students in shopping for the best price on materials, we have included a list of science catalogs that can be accessed online.

Catalogs

Catalogs are often an overlooked reading resource in the classroom. Science supply catalogs are powerful question engines, inspiring a multitude of new science inquiries. Catalogs are also great sources of ideas for materials that will aid students in their investigations. For authenticity in science, there's nothing more real than a science investigator ordering the materials needed from a catalog, especially

continued

with funds from an inquiry grant. Listed are companies that can provide interesting catalogs to place in the classroom.

Acorn Naturalists
www.acornnaturalists.com

American Science and Surplus
www.sciplus.com

Carolina Biological Supply Company
www.carolina.com

Delta Education
www.delta-education.com

Edmund Scientifics
www.scientificsonline.com

Educational Innovations
www.teachersource.com

Forestry Suppliers
www.forestry-suppliers.com

Science Is . . .
www.science-is.com

Sargent-Welch
www.sargentwelch.com

Ward's Natural Science
www.wardsci.com

Experts

KIC teachers often ask, "What do I do if my students settle on topics that I know nothing about?" The answer is, find someone who does know about it.

- Contact your local college or university for interested faculty and graduate students.
- Consider the topics that your students have chosen. Peruse your local yellow pages for companies and individuals who might contribute supplies or expertise.
- Your coworkers are likely to have hobbies, talents, and interests that you aren't aware of. Post a list of the areas of expertise that you are in need of.
- Send a note home to parents with specific career- or hobby-related needs.

- Remember that many students in your class may also be knowledgeable about topics chosen by others.

- Call or email KIC alumni and draw upon their KIC experiences.

Whenever possible, KIC teachers have invited various types of scientists into their classrooms. If that's not possible, you can still tap into their expertise by way of various ask-an-expert sites on the Internet (see samples below). If you or your students opt to use one of the ask-an-expert sites, there are several guidelines that will enable you to utilize these sites more effectively.

- Before you submit a question, familiarize yourself with the rules of that particular website.

- Make certain that you ask the right expert. Don't expect to get answers about chemistry from an astronomer.

- Many sites have question archives or FAQ sections. Check these first, to see if your question has already been answered.

- Do your research. Ask informed questions that illustrate some of what you have already learned.

- Include your age and/or grade level. This helps experts give grade-level-appropriate answers.

- Send a thank-you when your question has been answered. It will be greatly appreciated.

- Keep in mind that there is turnaround time involved. Most sites suggest that an answer should be expected within two weeks.

Ask-an-Expert Websites

Ask-a-Geologist (United States Geological Survey)
walrus.wr.usgs.gov/ask-a-geologist/
   Earth scientists field questions related to geologic features such as mountains, earthquakes, rocks, and volcanoes.

Ask a High Energy Astronomer (NASA's Goddard Space Flight Center)
imagine.gsfc.nasa.gov/docs/ask_astro/ask_an_astronomer.html
   Volunteers at the Laboratory for High Energy Astrophysics answer questions about X rays, gamma rays, and cosmic-ray astrophysics.

Ask a Marine Scientist
oceanlink.island.net/ask/askmain/ask.html

continued

Pose questions to marine scientists about marine vertebrates, marine invertebrates, marine ecology, biodiversity, oceanography, pollution, and the deep sea.

Ask an Astrobiologist (NASA Astrobiology Institute)
nai.arc.nasa.gov/astrobio/index.cfm
Astrobiologists provide feedback for your questions related to life on Earth, life on other planets, and planetary science.

Ask Dr. SOHO (NASA)
sohowww.nascom.nasa.gov (click on "Classroom" in lefthand list and then on "Ask Dr. SOHO")
Teams of NASA scientists answer your questions about the sun and SOHO, the Solar and Heliospheric Observatory.

Ask EPA (United States Environmental Protection Agency)
www.epa.gov/kids/ask.htm
Students can pose questions on any topic related to the environment.

Ask an Expert (National Wildlife Federation)
enature.com/expert/expert_home.asp
Different experts are available to provide guidance in all areas of wildlife and nature including insects and reptiles, gardening, birding, and plants.

Ask a Scientist (Howard Hughes Medical Institute)
www.hhmi.org/askascientist
Scientists from the Howard Hughes Medical Institute answer questions about various biology-related topics.

The MadSci Network
www.madsci.org/info/intro.html
This global effort relies on almost eight hundred experts to provide answers to your questions in engineering and all other fields of science.

Science Stock

A quick glance through past KIC projects does show that many students tend to have very minimal material needs. These needs are often for ordinary, everyday household items—straws, aluminum pans, paper cups, toothpicks—the types of things that you can find at your local discount or dollar store. Some of what you will want to keep on hand are throwaway items—empty liter bottles, paper towel rolls, empty jars, empty film canisters, and so forth. Following is a list of recommended materials to keep in stock for classroom inquiry.

Common Stock Materials Used for Classroom Inquiry

aluminum foil
plastic zippered bags and paper bags
assorted containers, preferably clear, both large and small
salt and baking soda
sand
balloons
seeds
cotton swabs and cotton balls
soil
dish detergent

straws
eyedroppers and small spoons
tongue depressors or Popsicle sticks
flashlights
food coloring
vegetable oil
magnets
vinegar
paper towels
waxed paper

Discovery Box Materials

Locating materials to fill the discovery boxes mentioned in Chapter 3 can be a daunting task. Common household items such as the ones listed previously are easy enough to procure, but where does one find UV beads and mealworms? Fortunately, Charles Pearce has provided information for some of his favorite suppliers of science materials.

Sources for Materials and Ideas

American Science and Surplus
3605 Howard Street
Skokie, IL 60076
Huge variety of inexpensive and hard to locate items
www.sciplus.com

Educational Innovations
151 River Road
Cos Cob, CT 06807
Ultraviolet-detecting beads and other items suited for inquiry
www.teachersource.com

Edmund Scientifics
101 East Gloucester Pike
Barrington, NJ 08007
www.scientificsonline.com

continued

Carolina Biological Supply Company
2700 York Road
Burlington, NC 27215
www.carolina.com

Tops Learning Systems
10970 South Mulino Road
Canby, OR 97013
Wide range of inquiry science activity ideas
www.topscience.org

Acorn Naturalists
PO Box 2423
Tustin, CA 92781
Materials for exploring the outdoors
www.acornnaturalists.com

Budgets are always tight. Materials can also be gathered from forgotten storage closets, parents, the local dollar store, donations from local businesses, and discarded items at the end of each school year.

Resource Sets

Over the years, we have noticed that there are some KIC topics that seem to be perennial favorites—bacteria, plants, pet behavior, and consumer testing, to name a few. These common interests are in your favor, as you can actually anticipate some of the topics that your students will choose, and you can gather your resources in advance. Perhaps you could create resource sets, like the one below, for the most common KIC topics. Then, many of your resources will already be available when you and your students need them.

Resource Set for "Things That Go"

Books

Ardley, Neil. 1992. *The Science Book of Machines*. San Diego, CA: Harcourt Brace Jovanovich.
> Photographs and clear instructions illustrate and demonstrate the step-by-step methods by which eleven simple machines can be built.

Bendick, Jeanne. 1992. *Eureka! It's an Automobile*. Brookfield, CT: Millbrook.

continued

A question-and-answer format and colorful, cartoonlike illustrations invite readers to share in the experiences of an automobile inventor.

Graham, Ian. 1993. *Boats, Ships, Submarines and Other Floating Machines*. New York: Kingfisher.
Color drawings and cutaway diagrams accompany descriptions of various floating machines and explanations of what makes them float.

———. 1993. *Cars, Bikes, Trains, and Other Land Machines*. New York: Kingfisher.
Learn about wheels, brakes, and concepts such as locomotion and suspension in this book about land machines.

Jennings, Terry. 1993. *Planes, Gliders, Helicopters, and Other Flying Machines*. New York: Kingfisher.
Air pressure and gravity are two of the concepts addressed in this book, which focuses on how flying machines work.

Kentley, Eric. 1992. *Boat*. New York: Random House.
The easy-to-read text, up-close photographs, and detailed diagrams in this book explore a variety of boats, and there's even a section on how to sail a boat.

Kerrod, Robin. 1992. *Amazing Flying Machine*. New York: Knopf/Random House.
This introductory look at flying machines is filled with color photographs and drawings to help illustrate various kinds of flying machines, how they work, and what they do.

Lafferty, Peter. 1992. *Force and Motion*. New York: Dorling Kindersley.
Floating and sinking, weight and mass, pressure and flow, gravity, friction, motion, and force are explored in this look at where machines get their power.

Lampton, Christopher. 1991. *Bathtubs, Slides, Roller Coaster Rails: Simple Machines That Are Really Inclined Planes*. Brookfield, CT: Millbrook.
This look at simple machines focuses on machines that are inclined planes and explains just how friction and gravity factor into how they work.

Macaulay, David. 1998. *The New Way Things Work*. Boston: Houghton Mifflin.
This updated look at the world of machines, and how they work, features line drawings and easy-to-understand text.

continued

Pinna, Simon de. 1998. *Forces and Motion*. Raintree Steck-Vaughn.
Readers can learn about some of the forces that make their vehicles go.

Rinard, Judith E. 2001. *The Book of Flight: From the Smithsonian's National Air and Space Museum*. Buffalo, NY: Firefly.
This book, with its timeline, colorful photos, and chronological presentation, is a good choice for students who are researching the history of flight.

Simon, Seymour. 1971. *The Paper Airplane Book*. New York: Viking.
Find out how to construct all kinds of paper airplanes and learn how to keep your plane in the air.

Sobey, Ed. 2002. *How to Build Your Own Prize-Winning Robot*. Berkeley Heights, NJ: Enslow.
Students who want to move beyond more simply constructed machines might be interested in reading how they could design and build their own robot.

Wyler, Rose. 1986. *Science Fun with Toy Boats and Planes*. New York: Simon and Schuster.
Build boats and planes to explore friction, equal-and-opposite reactions, weight, lift, and gravity.

Zubrowski, Bernie. 1985. *Raceways! Having Fun with Balls and Trucks*. New York: William Morrow/HarperCollins.
Step-by-step instructions help you build raceways, and a special section of the book explains the physical properties associated with each of the raceways and their accompanying activities.

———. 1986. *Wheels at Work: Building and Experimenting with Models and Machines*. New York: William Morrow/HarperCollins.
Wheels are vital to many machines, and in this book, there are step-by-step instructions for a number of models and machines as well as explanations for how and why they work.

Websites

Aeronautics—Principles of Flight
www.allstar.fiu.edu/aero/princ1.htm
The principles of flight are explained, and by learning about the parts of an airplane and their functions, students will have a better understanding of what it takes to get their own flying machines airborne.

continued

Alex's Paper Airplanes
www.paperairplanes.co.uk/
> With its variety of paper airplanes, and instructions for making them, this site is a good choice for those students who are interested in exploring various aspects and variables related to the design and flight capabilities of paper airplanes.

Amusement Park Physics: What Are the Forces Behind the Fun?
www.learner.org/exhibits/parkphysics/
> Students interested in working with raceways and ramps would benefit from this site, which looks at the forces and physics of amusement park rides, including roller coasters.

Fear of Physics. Physics. Explained. Finally.
www.fearofphysics.com
> Speed and acceleration, gravity, potential energy, straight-line motion, and friction are a few of the concepts explained at this site, which will help get those vehicles started and keep them in motion.

HowStuffWorks
www.howstuffworks.com
> At this site, electric cars, magler trains, segways, airplanes, blimps, and bicycles are among the things that go that are explained.

How Things Fly
www.aero.hq.nasa.gov/edu/
> Cartoon drawings help illustrate how things such as airplanes, spacecraft, and balloons are able to fly.

Inventor's Toolbox: The Elements of Machines
www.mos.org/sln/Leonardo/InventorsToolbox.html
> Examine the different elements of machines before putting your newfound knowledge to the Gadget Anatomy test.

The Virtual Kite Zoo
www.kites.org/zoo/
> Learn kite terminology, how to make kites, and how to fly them. There's even a bit of kite history.

Experts

engineers	mechanics
ship builders	electricians
hobbyists	

continued

Materials

paper clips	rubber bands
assorted types of tape	heavy cardboard
(masking, electrical, adhesive)	balsa wood
assorted plastic containers	thread spools
(empties from yogurt, deli	milk cartons
salads, margarine)	styrofoam pieces
glue	wooden dowels
various sizes and weights of	thread
paper (copy paper,	fabric pieces
construction paper, cardstock)	plastic liter bottles
paper towel tubes	

The recommendations and suggestions that we have shared in this chapter are merely a sampling of resources that could prove useful to you and your students. You are certain to already have some resources in place. Others will be sought and discovered as you and your students explore and research their unique questions.

Appendices

The following forms, which have been referenced within the book, may be copied for classroom use and are also available to download from *Beyond the Science Fair's* companion website at *www.heinemann.com/beyondthescience fair*. They are arranged alphabetically so they may be found easily.

A. Application for Hands-on Display

B. Application for Presentation

C. Biographical Data Form

D. Certificate of Participation

E. Chaperone Letter

F. Checklist for Host Institution

G. Checklist for Teachers

H. Congratulations and Acceptance Letter

I. Inquiry Grant Proposal Application

J. Journal Article Guidelines

K. KIC Is Coming Announcement

L. Moderator Letter

M. Parents' Guide to KIC

N. Parent Survey

O. Participant (Student) Survey

P. Presentation Blurb Guidelines

Q. Presentation Evaluation Form

R. Presentation Guidelines

S. Progress Report

T. Publicity Announcement

U. Teacher-Student Contract

V. Inquiry Investigation Plan

Application for Hands-On Display

The Kids' Inquiry Conference

The Kids' Inquiry Conference Committee is interested in providing a variety of hands-on activities at KIC. Students and adults learn best by doing. The KIC Committee would like to invite you to plan and operate a hands-on activity. Please complete the spaces below.

Name _____ Date _____

School _____

Teacher _____ Grade _____

Partners You Plan to Work With: _____

_____

1. Describe any reports or projects that you have prepared for science class in the past two years.

    _____

    _____

    _____

    _____

2. List any science articles or booklets that you have published in recent years (such as class or school magazine or newspaper).

    _____

    _____

    _____

    _____

3. List two or three discoveries you have made within the past two years, either at school or elsewhere.

    _____

    _____

    _____

    _____

4. Describe the hands-on activity that you would like to offer at KIC. What will be the topic?

    _____

    _____

_____

_____

5. Explain what visitors will do at your hands-on activity.

_____

_____

_____

_____

6. List the materials you plan to have available at your hands-on activity.

_____

_____

_____

_____

7. What do you hope visitors to your hands-on activity will learn?

_____

_____

_____

_____

Please sign below if you are willing to participate in the hands-on portion of the Kids' Inquiry Conference. Your application will be reviewed by the KIC Committee and you will be notified of the committee's decision.

_____

Signature of Applicant

_____

Signature of Parent

_____

Signature of Teacher

Thank you and good luck!

Application for Presentation

The Kids' Inquiry Conference

The Kids' Inquiry Conference Committee is eager to hear about your scientific research and discoveries. In order to plan the conference, your assistance is needed. Please complete the spaces below.

Name _____ Date _____

Co-presenters' names _____

School _____

Teacher _____ Grade _____

1. Describe any reports or projects that you have prepared for science class in the past two years.

    _____

    _____

    _____

2. List any science articles or booklets that you have published in recent years (such as class or school magazine or newspaper).

    _____

    _____

    _____

3. List two or three discoveries you have made within the past two years, either at school or elsewhere.

    _____

    _____

    _____

    _____

4. Describe the question you are researching and would like to present at KIC.

    _____

    _____

    _____

    _____

5. Briefly discuss your investigation. What are you doing to attempt to answer your question?

    _____

    _____

    _____

    _____

6. How is your research progressing? How would you evaluate the success of your investigation thus far?

    _____

    _____

    _____

    _____

7. What will you include in your presentation to convince your audience that your discoveries are valid?

    _____

    _____

    _____

    _____

Please sign below if you are willing to present your findings at the Kids' Inquiry Conference. Your application will be reviewed by the KIC Committee and you will be notified of the committee's decision.

_____

Signature of Applicant

_____

Signature of Teacher

_____

Signature of Parent

The Kids' Inquiry Conference
Presenter's Biographical Data Form

Directions to presenters:

A. Complete the spaces on this form.

B. Give this form to the moderator in your presentation room at the conference.

Your Name _____ Age _____ Grade _____

Teacher _____ School _____

School Activities _____

Hobbies _____

Favorite Books _____

How did you get interested in scientific research? _____

_____

_____

List one or more of your accomplishments. _____

_____

_____

What other science questions have you investigated? _____

_____

_____

What are your hopes for the future? _____

_____

_____

Why did you decide to present your investigation and discoveries at the Kids' Inquiry Conference?

_____

_____

Thank you for participating in the Kids' Inquiry Conference!

Certificate of Achievement

Awarded to

_____

this _____ **day of** _____

for participation in the

Kids' Inquiry Conference

presented by

_____

Dear Chaperone:

We are delighted that you will be accompanying your child's class to the Kids' Inquiry Conference at [insert location] on [insert date]. It promises to be a grand day of science, sharing, learning, and fun!

We are expecting [insert number of classes/students], their teachers, principals, and special guests, and members of the press. The keynote speaker will be [insert keynote speaker's name].

This promises to be a very busy day and we need your help! Your child's teacher may assign you to a specific task, but we ask that all parents be on the lookout for the well-being of each and every child at the conference.

Here are a few things to keep in mind while attending KIC.

- The main purpose of the breakout sessions is for children to share their scientific research and hear about the research of others. There will be a moderator in each session, but feel free to join in. You might want to ask questions that help students draw connections among the various presentations in the session.

- If you are in a breakout session, please check that all students are able to see and hear. Children (both presenters and audience) should enter the rooms first and sit up front. Adults can then fill in the rear and sides of the room.

- All students and adults will bring their own lunch. There will be several trash cans around the room for everyone to dispose of their own trash. Please help us to keep the room clean.

- Above all, *have fun*! This is a great opportunity to see young scientists in action!

Once again, thank you for your interest in the Kids' Inquiry Conference. We look forward to meeting you and hope you have as much fun as your student scientists.

Sincerely,

[Insert name/s]
The KIC Committee

KIC Checklist for Host Institutions

___ Decide upon location and date for conference and reserve location.

___ Send mailing to teachers and school systems about KIC and schedule informational meeting.

___ Prepare materials and agenda for informational meeting.

___ Send out commitment notices and deadlines dates.

___ Organize the KIC calendar of important dates and deadlines. Distribute to participating teachers.

___ Arrange keynote speaker, if desired.

___ Type and distribute the KIC announcement to participating teachers.

___ Collect class lists and information about classes for KIC planning.

___ Collect all presentation blurbs to organize sessions.

___ Plan sessions based upon presentation topics.

___ Prepare scheduling sheets and distribute to each class.

___ Remind teachers to have students complete their biographical data forms.

___ Seek moderators to preside at each presentation session.

___ Notify media.

___ Brief moderators.

___ Collect all journal articles.

___ Prepare master copies of the *KIC Journals* for distribution on the day of the conference.

___ Prepare color-coded name tags for each student based upon sign-up sheets.

___ Make bus parking arrangements.

___ Schedule workers and assign tasks for the day of the conference.

___ Prepare room signs showing color code and presentation title for each session.

___ Prepare KIC program for distribution at the conference.

___ Prepare certificates for distribution.

___ Do signs for lunch storage.

___ Set up welcome table.

___ Prepare rooms and check audiovisual equipment.

On the day of the conference:

___ Direct students to proper presentation rooms, based on color-coded name tags.

___ Assist moderators (gather bio sheets, review procedures for sessions).

___ Assist student presenters with setup.

___ Distribute KIC certificates and goodie bags.

KIC Checklist for Teachers

___ Decide that you and your students would like to participate in a Kids' Inquiry Conference.

___ Launch students into authentic investigations that attempt to answer testable questions.

___ Secure bus transportation.

___ Have students complete applications to present at KIC, either the entire class or only students interested in presenting. Also make sure applications for hands-on displays are completed.

___ Evaluate applications to present. Return those in need of additional information.

___ Send acceptance letters with guidelines for presenting and preparing hands-on demonstrations.

___ Send letters to parents explaining KIC or host a parent meeting.

___ Have student presenters write blurbs that briefly describe presentations. Blurbs will be included in schedule and sign-up sheets.

___ Have the students rehearse presentations for one another and/or other students at school. Help them revise and adapt per audience response.

___ Distribute and gather parent permission slips/consent forms for trip permission and photo release.

___ Have students complete presentation articles for inclusion in the *KIC Journal*. Journal articles should be typed in Word.

___ Have students sign up for desired presentation sessions.

___ Notify media.

___ Arrange for chaperones.

___ Distribute letters to chaperones and/or moderators.

___ Have presenters prepare biography sheets for use by moderators. These are to be taken to the conference.

___ Have presenters prepare packing checklists for presentation materials to take to KIC.

___ Attend your Kids' Inquiry Conference.

___ Have students complete KIC survey.

___ Arrange for adult volunteers to copy and assemble *KIC Journals*, if needed.

On the day of the conference:

___ Assist students and chaperones with check-in and directions to rooms as needed.

___ Assist moderators (gather bio sheets, provide any special instructions).

___ Assist student presenters with setup.

___ Distribute KIC certificates and other materials.

To: *Date:*

Congratulations ! ! !

Your application to present at the Kids' Inquiry Conference has been accepted by the KIC Committee. We are excited about your research and look forward to your presentation.

To plan your presentation, please consider the following guidelines.

1. Review again the *exact* question you tried to answer.

2. Read through the notes and records you kept during your research. Review *exactly* what you did to answer your question.

3. Think about the results of your investigation. Was your question answered? If not, can you explain what happened? If yes, will you be able to convince others that your results are valid?

4. Plan your presentation. It should include

   - your original question

   - what others have discovered about similar or related questions

   - a description of your investigation (photographs, diagrams, or charts will be helpful)

   - the results of your investigation—your discoveries (charts, graphs, and/or tables will make your results more convincing)

   - additional questions that might be interesting to pursue later by you or others

When you present, try to relax. Speak slowly and loudly enough for everyone to hear. *Repeat for your audience any questions asked by individual students.*

   Your class and teacher are proud of you. All of us thank you for your willingness to share your discoveries with other student scientists!

PLEASE SHOW THIS LETTER TO YOUR PARENTS. A PERMISSION SLIP AND ADDITIONAL INFORMATION EXPLAINING THE DETAILS OF THE KIDS' INQUIRY CONFERENCE WILL BE SENT HOME SOON!

Inquiry Grant Proposal Application

Students who are engaged in, or are planning, a scientific investigation are invited to apply for financial assistance to further their research. The Inquiry Grant Committee is interested in all areas of scientific inquiry. Please describe your investigation by completing the spaces below.

Names of Students Working Together on This Project _____

_____

Teacher(s) _____ Grade Level _____ Date _____

Describe the testable question that this research will attempt to answer.

_____

_____

_____

_____

Budget—List the materials needed, the quantities, the approximate costs, and the sources.

MATERIALS	QUANTITY	APPROXIMATE COST	SOURCE
_____	_____	_____	_____
_____	_____	_____	_____
_____	_____	_____	_____
_____	_____	_____	_____
_____	_____	_____	_____

TOTAL AMOUNT OF GRANT REQUEST $_____

Describe how your group plans to use the materials to answer the question. (Provide a step-by-step procedure.)

_____

_____

_____

_____

_____

_____

_____

_____

Provide a schedule of your project. (Include start date, major milestones, and completion date.)

_____

_____

_____

_____

_____

Describe your plans for evaluating the success of your investigation. (How will you know if you are successful?)

_____

_____

_____

_____

_____

Has your group applied for, or received financial support from other sources? If so, please describe.

_____

_____

_____

If this grant request is approved, a written report will be required upon completion of the project. The report is to describe the testable question, materials used for the investigation, how the investigation was conducted, and the results of the investigation.

By signing this grant request, the students agree to the provisions described and indicate that the information contained in this application is accurate.

_____

_____

_____

_____

SIGNATURES OF STUDENT SCIENTISTS

*A RESPONSE TO THIS GRANT REQUEST WILL BE PROVIDED
WITHIN TWO TO THREE WEEKS.*

Planning and Writing Your *KIC Journal* Article

In addition to your presentation, you will write an article about your KIC research, which will be published in the *KIC Journal* and on the KIC website. Think about your article as the story of your questions, investigation, and discoveries. This is your opportunity to share your work with those who might not see your presentation but are interested in your investigation. Future generations of KIC participants may be inspired by your work, so include enough details for others to understand what you did and what you learned.

Guidelines for What to Include in Your Journal Article

Article title and authors

- Record the title of your investigation and the names of the members of your research group.

Questions/topic

- What is the topic of your investigation?
- How did you become interested in this topic?
- What specific question(s) did you explore during your investigation?

Background information

- What background information did you learn about your topic that is interesting and important to understand related to the focus of your investigation?

Your investigation

- What did you do to investigate your question(s)?
- Use your scientist's notebook to summarize important events or moments in your investigation from the very beginning to the end.

Discoveries

- Share what you learned from your investigation.
- What were your successes and failures?
- What surprised you?

Next steps

- What new questions do you have as a result of your investigation that could be investigated in the future?

Resources

- Record the resources you used to conduct your investigation (books, interviews, journal articles, etc.).

Illustrations/tables/charts

- You may include any data you wish to share related to your article.

Remember, this article will be published, so proofread and edit your work carefully.

KIC is coming!

Our class has been invited to attend the Kids' Inquiry Conference later this spring. KIC is an opportunity to

- meet with students from different schools
- share our own discoveries with others
- hear about the discoveries of other students
- discuss shared interests in science and research

How will our research be shared with others? Students are invited to prepare presentations in which they will tell about their own questions and what they did to answer their questions.

Who will attend the presentations? Other students with interests similar to yours will attend your presentation. They will be invited to ask questions and to comment on your research.

Am I required to present at KIC? No. Students who attend are not required to present. However, all are invited to prepare a presentation if they have engaged in original research of testable questions and are excited about their own discoveries.

What kind of research topics might be appropriate for KIC? Any testable question that you have actually investigated is a suitable topic. Questions answered through your own investigations are ideal. Other sources of investigation topics could be past *KIC Journal* articles, the question board, topics from science class (this or past years), or books you have been reading.

If I decide to present, what should my presentation include? First, you will want to share with your audience the question that you investigated. Then you will tell about your adventures of discovery: what you did to answer your question and what you discovered from your research. A question-and-answer period will follow your presentation, in which your audience will be invited to discuss your investigation and discoveries.

How will I decide which presentations to attend at the conference? A listing of presentation topics and presenters will be published before the conference. Students may sign up for those presentations that seem interesting to them.

I really want to present at KIC! What do I do now? Tell your teacher! Gather your data and prepare for the big day. You will receive an application to present that will be sent to and reviewed by the KIC Committee. Then, if your application is selected, you will become an official Kids' Inquiry Conference presenter.

Have a wonderful day at KIC!

The Kids' Inquiry Conference
Moderating KIC Sessions

Thank you for agreeing to moderate a research and sharing session at the Kids' Inquiry Conference. Here are a few tips concerning the role of the moderator.

KIC was designed so that kids could experience sharing the excitement of their science research with their peers. These sharing sessions are the heart of the conference.

Most sessions will have presentations from three groups of student scientists. Some of the children have been in touch with one another. Others will be unfamiliar with the research of their fellow presenters.

Each session will be thirty minutes long. The structure of the sessions is flexible but should include the following:

- The moderator will introduce the student presenters (don't forget to introduce yourself as well).
- Each student/group will present their research.
- Each student/group should have equal time to present (approximately seven minutes).
- There should be time allotted for questions and discussion after each presentation.

1. Introduce each group of scientists. You may be given a brief biography of each child. If not, get their names and the names of their schools in advance.
2. Establish a sense of order and monitor time. You are in charge of the session. It *must* be completed in thirty minutes. Make sure everyone gets a turn to present.
3. Help with audiovisual equipment. Students may be using overheads, slides, and VCRs. All equipment will be in the room.
4. Ask, "Where do we go from here?" Encourage students to think about what new questions they have after the presentation, how they could explore these questions, and/or how they could help one another's research.
5. *Do not let children leave early, but please have everyone ready to leave at the end of the session.* Time is very tight. There will only be five minutes between sessions.

There will be plenty of parents, chaperones, teachers, and staff around. Feel free to use their help with discussions, questions, equipment, bathrooms, errands, timing, and so on.

Thank you for helping to make KIC a success!

Parents' Guide to the Kids' Inquiry Conference

The Kids' Inquiry Conference is an opportunity for children to present discoveries made during scientific investigations based upon original questions. This guide is designed to help parents who are curious about how to best assist their children.

How did the children select the questions being investigated?

Students have been invited to select their own testable questions. A testable question is one that can best be answered by designing an experiment or by conducting observations. Sources of questions have been from our science units, books students have been reading, science articles written by students in past years, and experiences at school and elsewhere. Your child selected a particular question of special interest.

How can I best assist my child during the investigation and planning for the conference?

Since the question selected by your child is one of particular interest, he or she is curious about finding an answer on his or her own. Minimal guidance from parents may be helpful, but permitting space for the child to investigate and gather data on his or her own is an important part of the scientific process.

As your child plans for the conference, please

Do	Do Not
• be available for guidance *if* your your child should need your help	• change or revise the question being investigated
• ask questions about your child's investigation and how it is progressing	• offer advice beyond that sought by your child
• be ready to supply materials that your child may need for the investigation the conference	• gather data, make posters, write the article, or prepare the presentation
• help your child schedule meetings with partners	• arrange partners for your child
• trust your child's judgment as he/she investigates the question	• attempt to make the investigation more than your child originally planned

On the day of the conference, please

Do	Do Not
• plan to visit and see your child's presentation or hands-on activity	• sit in the front of the presentation rooms
• help with carrying of materials, setup and cleanup	• ask questions following presentations before student participants have asked theirs
• have lunch with the students	• help your child with the presentation or with the answering of questions
• visit other presentations and hands-on activities	• assist behind the hands-on tables
• take photographs	

Thank you for your assistance in helping to make the Kids' Inquiry Conference a success!

KIC Parent Survey

Thank you for joining us today at the Kids' Inquiry Conference. Please help us by responding to the questions below.

Your Name _____

Your Child's Name _____

Your Child's School _____

Check the statements below that apply.

My child:

_____ presented at KIC today

_____ provided a hands-on table experience today

_____ participated in the audience at KIC today

_____ is a scientist

_____ enjoys doing science investigations

_____ has been motivated by the possibilities of KIC

_____ has been talking about KIC a lot at home

_____ will probably continue his or her investigation(s) after KIC

What did you especially like about KIC as a field trip?

How could next year's conference be improved?

Additional comments about the conference:

May we use what you have written in future publications about KIC?

Thank you for your assistance!

KIC Participant Survey

The KIC Committee hopes you enjoyed your day at the Kids' Inquiry Conference. To help plan next year's conference, please complete this survey.

Your Name _____ School _____

(Circle Yes or No) Did you visit the KIC website?   Yes   No

(Circle any that apply) I was a   presenter   hands-on participant

1. What did you do to prepare for KIC?

2. Did preparing for and attending KIC make you a better scientist? How do you know?

3. How has your thinking about being a scientist changed because of KIC?

4. Describe your favorite part of The Kids' Inquiry Conference.

5. Describe any new interests you have because of KIC.

6. Would you recommend the Kids' Inquiry Conference to others? Why or why not?

7. What changes can you suggest to make KIC better next year?

KIC Presentation Description Guide:
Writing Your Blurb

The KIC Committee is pleased that your presentation has been accepted for this year's Kids' Inquiry Conference. Among your responsibilities will be to write a short description of your presentation (about thirty-five words or less). The description you write will be used to help other students decide which presentations they would like to attend.

Presentation descriptions, also called *blurbs*, are like advertisements. They should be clever and snappy, yet truthful. Read the blurbs below from past years.

A Moldy Experience

What grows on cheese, bread, and juice?
It's *mold* and it's on the loose!
Come see for yourself.

Mealworms: The Uninvited Visitors for Breakfast

What do you do if you can't find information
on a bug you like? Research it yourself!
See how a group of students gathered data about
this interesting creature.

Would these blurbs attract you? Think about why or why not.

Now think about your own blurb. Talk about some ideas with one or two friends. Try to write a description that you think will make people want to attend *your* presentation.

Blurbs will be due on _____.

KIC Presentation Evaluation

Presenter _____

Topic _____ Date _____

Please circle one number for each item.

Rate how well the presenter(s):	effective			not effective
1. described their question(s)	3	2	1	0
2. shared background information on their topic	3	2	1	0
3. explained the investigation	3	2	1	0
4. told about their discoveries	3	2	1	0
5. suggested questions for future students	3	2	1	0
6. used charts, graphs, and diagrams to show data	3	2	1	0

7. Did you find the presentation convincing? Why or why not?

8. What do you think was especially *good* about the presentation?

9. How could this presentation be improved?

10. What additional question(s) do you still have about this topic?

Thank you for your responses!

KIC Presentation Guidelines

Preparation

1. Prepare a brief outline or overview of your presentation. Include an introduction of your group, the question you investigated, methods of investigation, findings from your investigation, and next steps or new questions.
2. Your presentation time is ten minutes, but you need to leave time at the end for audience questions (two to three minutes).
3. Divide your presentation among your group members.
4. Prepare brief notes or talking points for the information you will present. Practice this information without relying too heavily on notes.
5. Prepare visual aids and materials for your presentation. Practice using the visuals as you speak.
6. Prepare any handouts or materials for the audience. You will need forty copies for the audience.
7. Store and organize your presentation materials in your inquiry box, clearly labeled with your names and the name of your project.

General Presentation Skills

1. Use a clear, loud voice.
2. Speak slowly, not too fast.
3. Look at the audience—don't put your head down.
4. Use visuals when appropriate.

Practice Tips

1. The more you practice, the more comfortable you will be with your presentation in front of an audience.
2. Rehearse in front of a mirror, your family, and your group. You will also be able to practice in front of an audience in school.
3. Tape-record or videotape your presentation and play it back in order to monitor your rate and volume of speech.
4. Relax and smile. You're going to give a wonderful presentation!

KIC Progress Report

Name _____ Date _____

The KIC Committee is interested in the progress of your plans for KIC. Please tell
about your progress by completing the spaces below.

1. Are you doing a presentation, hands-on display, or both? _____

2. What is your topic? _____

3. So far, what have you accomplished? _____

    _____

    _____

    _____

    _____

4. Describe any difficulties you are having (unable to get materials, problems
    with partners, not enough time, etc.).

    _____

    _____

    _____

    _____

5. If KIC were to be held tomorrow, would you be ready? YES NO

6. If *no*, list the things you still have to do to get ready.

    _____

    _____

    _____

    _____

7. On a scale of 0 to 10 (with 0 being perfectly calm), how nervous are you
    about KIC?

    (circle one) 0 1 2 3 4 5 6 7 8 9 10

8. How many days remain until KIC? _____

Thank you for your answers!

[Insert name of school or host]
announces the

Kids' Inquiry Conference

[Insert Date]
[Insert Location]

- [Insert teacher's name] students, [insert school]
-
-
-

KIC Goals

The goals of the Kids' Inquiry Conference are to provide students with opportunities to

- share the excitement of their own discoveries
- interact with students from different schools who share common interests
- view science as a dynamic force in their own lives
- critically consider the credibility of their own research and the research of others
- draw upon the discoveries of other students to enhance their own research

Program

The primary emphasis of the Kids' Inquiry Conference is on children sharing their own science research with other children. The program is designed to be as close to a scientific conference as possible and may include a combination of the following activities:

- panel and/or poster sessions in which students share their own research and hear about the research of other students
- hands-on workshops
- a variety of science-related tours
- featured speakers
- opportunities to establish ongoing contact among participants

continued

Transportation

Each teacher will make travel arrangements for his or her own class.

Lunch

KIC participants will bring their own lunches to the conference.

Chaperones

Each class will be accompanied by a minimum of (insert number) chaperones, but teachers are welcome to bring as many parent volunteers as they wish. Chaperones will be asked to perform specified duties.

Publicity

Because participating schools are very excited about the unique nature of the Kids' Inquiry Conference, we will be notifying local media and national educational and science organizations about the program. Therefore, in addition to school permission forms, parents or guardians will be asked to sign photo release forms. Children who do not have signed release forms *will fully participate* in the day's activities. We will do our best to make sure that these children are not photographed, but we cannot make any guarantees.

Moderators

Each breakout session is assigned a moderator to introduce presenters and keep the conversation active. Parents, teachers, and school personnel will serve as moderators.

Questions? For further information, ask participating teachers or contact:

> [Insert coordinator's name]
> [Insert coordinator's contact information]

TEACHER-STUDENT
CONTRACT

CONTRACT NUMBER _____

DATE_____

_____ agrees to work on the following long-term assignment:

CONDUCT A SCIENTIFIC INVESTIGATION
to be completed on or before _____

The classroom teacher agrees to provide a reasonable amount of class time by exempting the student from selected classroom assignments.

Completion of this contract (will / might / will not) require additional time at home.

The following provisions apply in the completion of this contract.

- The student will prepare a contract journal.
- The student will attempt to answer the following testable question:

_____

_____

- An *inquiry investigation plan* will be completed.
- Daily entries will be made in the contract journal in which activities, observations, data, sketches, and notes will be recorded.
- The results of the investigation will be recorded in the contract journal.
- Discoveries will be recorded in the *Book of Student Discoveries*.

The student agrees to do his or her best work on the completion of this contract.

_____
STUDENT

_____
PARENT

_____
TEACHER

CLASS ____

Inquiry Investigation Plan

Name _____ Date _____

I am interested in (topic) _____

I would like to attempt to answer the following testable question:

_____

_____

I predict that _____

_____

The following materials will be needed for my investigation.

MATERIAL	SOURCE	MATERIAL	SOURCE
_____	_____	_____	_____
_____	_____	_____	_____
_____	_____	_____	_____

To answer my question, I will do the following:

(First) _____

_____

_____

(Next) _____

_____

_____

_____

(Then) _____

_____

_____

_____   Sketch (with labels)

I will need ___ school hours per week, and ___ home hours per week for my investigation. My investigation will take approximately ___ weeks to complete.

Teacher Notes:

Contributors

Wendy Saul serves as the Shopmaker Professor of Education at the University of Missouri–St. Louis. She is editor in chief of *Thinking Classroom: An International Journal of Reading Writing and Critical Reflection*, published by the International Reading Association and author or editor of a number of books about the science-literacy connection, including *Vital Connections: Children, Science, and Books* (Heinemann 1991), *Beyond the Science Kit* (Heinemann 1996), *Science Workshop: Reading, Writing, and Thinking Like a Scientist* (Heinemann 2002), and *Crossing Borders in Literacy and Science Instruction: Perspectives on Theory and Practice* (IRA/NSTA 2004). As director of the National Science Foundation–supported Elementary Science Integration Projects, she has a special interest in helping educators create reading and writing activities that inform and are informed by science She is also the originator of *Search It! Science: The Books You Need at Lightning Speed* (*searchit.heinemann.com*), a web database program that suggests appropriate science titles for young readers, their teachers, and librarians.

Donna Dieckman, program director for the Elementary Science Integration Projects at the University of Maryland, Baltimore County (UMBC), works with classroom teachers, administrators, and university researchers on programs designed to support science and literacy connections. During her nine years as a classroom teacher, she became a strong advocate of using children's literature in the classroom. She has served as a member of the National Science Teachers Association Children's Book Council joint panel that selects the Outstanding Science Tradebook Awards in children's literature. She contributed a chapter to *Beyond the Science Kit* (Heinemann 1996) and is a coauthor of *Science Workshop: Reading, Writing, and Thinking Like a Scientist* (Heinemann 2002).

Charles Pearce is a resource teacher in the Extended Enrichment Program of the Carroll County, Maryland, school system. He is the recipient of the President's Award for Excellence in Science Teaching. Pearce is a lead teacher for the Elementary Science Integration Projects and a frequent presenter at regional and national conferences and workshops for teachers. He is the inspiration for the Kids' Inquiry Conference (KIC), which he has spearheaded for the past ten years, is the author of *Nurturing Inquiry: Real Science for the Elementary Classroom* (Heinemann 1999), and contributed a chapter to *Science Workshop: Reading, Writing, and Thinking Like a Scientist* (Heinemann 2002).

Donna Neutze is an assistant coordinator for the Center for Talented Youth at Johns Hopkins University. For seven years, she was the coordinator for the Elementary Science Integration Projects at the University of Maryland, Baltimore County. She oversaw the daily operations of *Search It! Science*, a database of outstanding children's science books, and she coordinated the Kids' Inquiry Conference. She contributed a chapter to *Science Workshop: Reading, Writing, and Thinking Like a Scientist* (Heinemann 2002) and has been a contributor to *Thinking Classroom*, a publication of the International Reading Association. She is currently enrolled in a Ph.D. program in language, literacy and culture and is pursuing her research interests in nonfiction children's literature and gender issues.

Megan Dieckman is a sophomore at Juniata College in Huntingdon, Pennsylvania, majoring in chemistry. Megan was a participant in the Kids' Inquiry Conference in the fourth grade. For the past five years, Megan has served as the student coordinator for KIC, meeting and communicating with students about their KIC experiences. She has been a presenter of workshops about the Kids' Inquiry Conference at several regional and national conferences. Megan hosts the "Ask Meg" section of the KIC website (*esiponline.learnserver.net/kic*), a forum for students to correspond about their questions, investigations, and preparation for presentations. Megan plans to pursue a career in elementary science education.